For [handwritten] with respect for all you inspire and educate us all! Julia Ingram [handwritten signature]

Born Scared

When Anxiety Was Created in the Womb, at Birth, or in Prior Lifetimes—and How Finding the Cause Leads to the Cure

Julia Ingram, MA, Hypnotherapist

Sibylline Press
Portland, Oregon

Ingram, Julia.

    Born Scared: when anxiety was created in the womb, at birth or in prior lifetimes—
and how discovering the cause leads to the cure
ISBN: 978-0-9899355-5-5

Psychology, Self-Help, Hypnosis, Anxiety, Fear, New Consciousness, Reincarnation

Author photo credit: Life Touch Portraits

1. Psychology and Self-Help 2. Anxiety 3. Hypnosis

Published by Sibylline Press
Portland, Oregon

Interior design produced by Booknook.biz.

Contents

Preface

Born Scared is about how the roots of most fears and anxiety can be discovered through the use of hypnosis, and that figuring out when, how, or under what conditions they were created makes them easier to resolve.

The title came to me as I was reading a fine book on treating anxiety by holistic psychiatrist Douglas Hunt. In the preface of *What Your Doctor May Not Tell You About Anxiety, Phobias, and Panic Attacks,* he wrote: "Granted, some of us are born anxious; and others become anxious as a result of situational stress or threat to one's life, property, or relationships."

Some people are born anxious. That's a significant statement and an issue to which I've given a lot of thought. Dr. Hunt said nothing more about those who were born anxious, but I realized I had a lot to say about it.

It is not enough for me to just treat symptoms. Plus, my clients want answers. Not knowing why you feel anxious or are fearful often adds to the problem and can make you feel hopeless. Who doesn't hate hearing "We don't know why"? It is insulting and demoralizing for a man suffering from a fear of enclosed spaces—such that he can't take the elevator to his tenth-floor office, let alone get on an airplane—to be told his fear is irrational. That is what traditional clinical psychology calls a phobia. Irrational. What he needs to hear is: "Let's find out."

Anxiety is an overall feeling of dread about something negative happening in the future, but not of a specific thing or event. It can be a physiological "felt sense" that may be the result of a hormone imbalance, the side effect of drugs (prescription and recreational), alcohol, or junk food. That type of anxiety should be treated physiologically. Anxiety can also have an emotional cause; it can be explored and reduced or eliminated via hypnotherapy.

Fear can be named. There's a fear of a person, a place, an event, an experience, a thing. Some fears show up as beliefs: "I'm unlovable, the world is a dangerous place, my anger is lethal, I always mess up," and on and on. If you believe you are unlovable, you will have a hard time recognizing love when it comes to you; if you believe the world is a dangerous place, you will notice what is dangerous and miss what is amazing. If you believe your anger is lethal, then you will suppress an important emotion—to your own and your intimates' detriment, and they will never fully know you. If you believe you'll always mess up, you probably mostly will.

If you know where the fear came from or why something isn't working, you can set about to find a solution. When you don't know why, there's nothing to work on except symptoms like negative thoughts, hypertension, difficulty sleeping, loss of appetite, or pain due to stress. Dealing only with symptoms usually means medication with all the attendant side effects or hours of cognitive or exposure therapy. While cognitive therapy has its place, in simple terms it is a masculine/left-brain approach. Change your thinking in a conscious way to triumph over your fears. The other school of thought is the feminine/right brain approach of hypnotherapy. Find the story buried in the subconscious and revise the story at its roots. I use both approaches, but I have found the feminine approach more effective in making deep and lasting changes.

The book is divided roughly into two parts. The first half is about children and adults who discovered their anxiety stemmed from experiences in the womb. We also look at how a difficult birth shapes one's worldview. Another chapter in the first half, "Womb Twin Survivors," is about the type of anxiety that comes from starting out life as a twin and then losing that sibling during gestation or soon after birth. Also covered are cases of fearful and anxious children, especially separation anxiety, night terrors, and panic attacks. These stories reveal prenatal, perinatal, and prior lifetime sources for the fears.

The second part of the book is about how eating disorders, including food aversions, phobias, social anxiety, and certain limiting beliefs were discovered as stemming from traumatic deaths in past lives. In chapter thirteen you'll learn that the archetypal themes from the "Burning Times"—the universal fears of being burned at the stake or banished from society—are quite common. Clients who felt called to be healers but found themselves blocked, or self-sabotaging the effort, discovered roots of these fears in past lives of being accused of witchcraft or heresy.

Besides the case studies from my private practice and some interviews, I also cite studies and claims from experts in the fields of biology, birth psychology, and psychiatry that back up certain statements I make; for instance, that a fetus can remember its conception (in some emotional or sensate form), that we do remember our birth experience, and that memories retrieved via hypnosis can be trusted.

The recovery process is covered in most of the cases, introducing you to a variety of healing options—some mainstream and some exciting new alternative treatments to explore with a professional.

In the mid-eighties, my own spiritual quest and curiosity about the concept of reincarnation led me to undergo a past-life regression. I found the experience personally fascinating, but also psychologically helpful. I already was using hypnosis with clients for relaxation, pain management, and to help them access childhood memories. It was quite easy to incorporate regressions into the work, after I received training in the process. I also attended classes and workshops through what is now known as the International Association for Regression Research and Therapies based in California. This association was founded by a group of clnical psychologists, social workers, and psychiatrists with highly respectable credentials. I appreciated the quality of the training and the courage of this group to think outside the box of traditional therapy. Using regression hypnosis has proven to be one of the best tools in my therapeutic toolbox when working with the types of cases described in this book.

Do I believe in reincarnation? Yes, I do. Do I understand how it works? Not really. What I know for certain is that there is a mechanism—I call it the high-wise self—within each human being which is a storyteller. It may be the same process that creates dreams or those welcome "aha" bursts of inspiration. When I lead my clients into a light-to-medium hypnotic state and prompt them to go to the source of a problem, this mechanism responds with an answer. Sometimes clients report a memory of a traumatic event from their current lifetime. Sometimes they report an image or metaphor, and we work it through by interpreting the message. But often my clients report scenes that they feel came from a different time and place—what we generally refer to as a past life. Do you need to believe in reincarnation to benefit from this book? Not at all. While those who think in those terms might find the concept easier, all you need to do is trust that you can tap into your own higher wisdom to access a story, an image, a knowing, a consciousness, that can explain your pain and lead to its resolution.

Some clients prefer to look at it from a transpersonal perspective, as in the collective unconscious or universal stories described by Carl G. Jung. And that works well. However my clients wish to interpret their experience, as long as it ends their suffering and increases their feelings of wellbeing and self-love, I'm satisfied.

The cases reported in this book are those of clients who, while seeking help for their own or their child's anxiety, discovered via regression therapy what they believed to be the cause. It was the discovery of the cause that led to its resolution. A connection that one client makes between his conception by rape and the belief that he should never have been born may not hold true for another client who was conceived in the same way. It will likely be affected by the violence, but if the infant is welcomed into the world and treated with love and kindness, there's no reason it can't live a rich, full, anxiety-free life. In other words, don't reverse the process and assume that the issues in the womb always cause the same problems. Not every child of an anxious or depressed mother will have problems; not every adoptee will have issues of low self-esteem or abandonment fears. Every person brings to each experience his or her own unique set of beliefs and perspective. That is what determines how a person will interpret whatever happens to them. And if you believe in reincarnation, you understand that many of those beliefs were formed in prior incarnations.

Like other books such as this one, some cases are composites; that is, I've combined two or more cases to make a more interesting story while others are from single cases or interviews. Names and other identifiers have been changed to protect each person's privacy. *Born Scared* is not specifically written for professionals working in the field of health or mental health. However, for anyone interested in page references to quotations in this book, please contact me. Born Scared isn't a self-help book because recovering from moderate to severe anxiety does require professional help. But I trust that these stories of courage and recovery will normalize what may have been judged as abnormal or unsympathetically called irrational. May they help you have more compassion and patience for yourself and others who suffer and inspire you to know it is possible to be free from fear and anxiety.

Chapter 1

A Shaky Beginning: Prenatal Trauma

One mother told me she was shocked to find her two-year-old daughter sitting on the living room floor chanting," Breathe in, breath out, breathe in, breathe out." The words were part of a Lamaze exercise the woman had practiced during the last weeks of her pregnancy. She had not uttered those words since.

Thomas R. Verny, MD,
Pre-Parenting: Nurturing Your Child from Conception

There is mounting evidence that everything a mother says, feels, and experiences during pregnancy is at some level experienced by her child. The little girl mentioned above certainly did. But just how much is remembered and to what degree is the child affected? It turns out to be considerable, as you will learn from a student of mine I call Deirdre.

For several years I offered a three-module training program in hypnotic regression techniques. Some of the classes were in my own city, but I also traveled to teach. It was Deirdre, a social worker, who invited me to come to her city. She had the local contacts and handled logistics such as enrollment and finding classroom space—in this case the commons area of a large condominium complex. It was much homier than a hotel and it was especially nice to take our breaks and have lunch by the pool during the five-day course of study. Deirdre and I met in person the first morning of the first class. She was tall, attractive, out-going, and as the attendees introduced themselves, she was animated as she expressed her excitement in anticipation of learning regression techniques.

After about an hour of lecture, I demonstrated a simple hypnotic induction and then broke the group into triads: one person to take the role of the subject (client), one the hypnotist (facilitator), and the third one would observe and take notes. The hypnotist had a script to follow: Physically relax the client, deepen the trance state, create an "inner workshop" in the mind's eye, give a post-hypnotic suggestion that he or she would get the most pos-sible from the training, and then bring the client out of the trance. The point of the exercise was to allow each of them to have the experience of putting someone into a light trance state, being the one put into the trance, or watch-ing the process. After the first practice round and people had changed roles, a facilitator, Karin, called me over.

"Deirdre doesn't think she can do this." My eager, out-going student was now huddled under a blanket, glassy-eyed and trembling. I put my hand on her shoulder and asked her to look at me. "Deirdre, what's going on?"

"I don't know. I really want to do this, and it went fine when I was Mike's facilitator, but when Karin told me to close my eyes and she started the induc-tion, I felt panicky. I'm sorry to be such a baby." She seemed embarrassed and a little ashamed that she was having trouble. After all it was she who had got-ten the ball rolling to bring me there—Deirdre obviously was motivated. But she wouldn't make it through the training if this wasn't resolved.

I reassured her that she wasn't the first student to have difficulties and that it was an opportunity for me to show her and the rest of the class how to work with people who react just as she had. Her color and breathing returned to normal. I told Mike to be the facilitator, Karin the subject, and Deirdre would observe.

"We'll take a break after this next round, and we can talk in private then." I handed Deirdre a bottle of water. She took a swig and gave the blanket to Mike.

At the break Deirdre and I talked. I asked if she had a history of trauma that might explain the hyper-vigilance. Clearly, she did not trust her sur-roundings enough to close her eyes. She shook her head. "I grew up in a loving family, no trauma, but I was sick a lot—allergies, irritable bowel syn-drome, and frequent throat infections." Those symptoms suggested problems with her immune system.

Intuitively (and because she had called herself a baby when she was trembling under the blanket), I asked what she knew about her birth. "Was it normal? Has your mother told you anything about it?" Her right hand flew to her chest.

"I'm dizzy," she gasped. She started to hyperventilate and her eyes went out of focus. Deirdre was heading for a panic attack, or at the very least she was dissociating, (a state in which some essential part of the person becomes separated or split off from the rest of the personality and may even func-tion independently). I took her hands in mine and asked her to match my breathing and she calmed down. Several people had brought snack food, so

I grabbed something from the kitchen for her to eat, which helped her get grounded back into her body.

"I'll just tell you what started running through my mind. When I was in high school, my mom told me when she was nine months pregnant with me, my father was almost killed. They were at a party. A motorcycle gang was messing with a friend of his who was sitting out front. My dad and mom went outside thinking the others from the party were coming to help too, but they didn't. My dad ended up being stabbed about twenty times." Since her pregnant mother was there during the attack, Deirdre was there too. I wanted to learn more.

Deirdre agreed to a regression to her mother's womb, and to doing it in front of the class. As she settled into the cushy overstuffed chair, I told her to feel the compassion and support of her close friend, Karin, and the other classmates who sat in a semicircle around her. I led her gently into the induction, reminding her that the process was safe and that she was safe. She was able to achieve a relaxed state, and when prompted to access a positive memory in her mother's womb, she smiled sweetly. "I feel her love for me." After allowing her a little time to remember feeling peace and love, I moved her forward to the moment of the attack.

"Panic, terror, anger, helplessness. This is just how I felt when Karin tried to get me deeper. Oh god!" She started to breathe harder.

"Deirdre, it is not happening now," I said. "You are safe." I instructed her to step out of the infant's memory and speak to me as an adult. Her breathing returned to normal. "Did your father survive the attack?" She said he had survived.

"And how is he doing today?"

"Really well."

"How is your mother today?"

"She's great too. They are both fine." She let out a huge breath as if letting go of a lifetime of worry. Those few minutes of severe trauma during the attack had been frozen in time within her subconscious mind. Until that memory was brought to the surface, there was only never-ending fear. Breaking through that time lock allowed her to see the present. The attack was long over with and her parents were fine. A good place to be.

All of the stress hormones Deirdre's mother secreted during those horrible moments had shot through the placenta and into the baby. Furthermore, Deirdre's own body responded to screams, shouts, and perceived danger and she had secreted her own fight-flight adrenal hormones. But trapped in the dark confining space of the womb, she could neither fight nor flee, but only freeze. It sounded like Deirdre remained swimming in that toxic pool.

If that overdose of hormones weren't enough, when I prompted her to look forward a few days, Deirdre reported feeling guilty that her mother's attention had to be divided between her and her father. She believed she was a *burden* to her mother, and useless to her father.

In her book, *Origins: How the Nine Months Before Birth Shape the Rest of Our Lives*, journalist Annie Murphy Paul wrote: "Much of what a pregnant woman encounters in her daily life—the air she breathes, the food and drink she consumes, the emotions she feels, the chemicals she's exposed to—are shared in some fashion with her fetus." She goes on to explain what happens in situations such as the one Deirdre experienced. She calls information from the mother "biological postcards from the world outside," answering questions critical to the baby's survival. "Will it be safe and protected, or will it face constant dangers and threats? Will it live a long, fruitful life, or a short, harried one?"

That fateful week, Deirdre came to believe that the world was a very dangerous place, and that violence could happen without warning.

"I was always full of adrenaline, expecting to be attacked at any moment. After school, or work, I'd run to my car. I was up at all hours of the night looking out the windows for an attacker, planning what I would do when they did attack."

She would tell herself there was no one outside, but her body was bracing for disaster. Fortunately for Deirdre, the trauma occurred in the ninth month. Had it occurred earlier, say between 28 to 32 weeks when her nervous systems were developing, I suspect the impact would have been much worse.

Now that we knew the source of her fear, it was time to begin the healing. While still in that relaxed trance state, I asked her to imagine her infant-self able to get rid of the flood of stress hormones, both her own and her mother's. In cases like this—a need to rid the body of a toxic memory—clients sometimes choose to imagine a cleansing bath or a shower under a beautiful waterfall. Some prefer to imagine the hormones, or the fearful energy, draining out of them. If they can't think of something, I'll help them create the healing ritual. Deirdre imagined bathing the infant in a fragrant warm bath.

Next, I suggested she show the infant that her parents are healthy and happy now and that it was time for her to focus on her own wellbeing. I also suggested that she see her world as a safe place, that she is safe, and there is no need to be vigilant against violence. Because her beliefs affected her brain cells, this process of changing her beliefs would begin to change her brain. As

Bruce Lipton, a leader in the field of New Biology and author of *The Biology of Belief* states: "Beliefs control biology! We have the capacity to consciously evaluate our responses to environmental stimuli and change old responses any time we desire . . . once we deal with the powerful subconscious mind.... We are not stuck with our genes or our self-defeating behaviors!" It was a good first step towards recovery for Deirdre.

A few weeks following the class, I asked her to describe what the regression revealed to her and she wrote:

> *The regression explained many of my odd behaviors as a child. I was always very sensitive and emotional, and careful to NEVER hurt anyone's feelings. I could not bear the thought of ever disappointing anyone. My father caused intense emotions in me. I was so affected by his very presence. He could walk in the room, and if he wasn't smiling I thought he must be disappointed in me, and immediately I would get a lump in my throat. If asked to talk, I'd burst into tears and I couldn't stop. This truly was so common as a child. My parents still talk about it to this day. As I grew, I learned to make people happy [as a way] to feel good about myself, or to feel worthy of being alive.*

Deirdre was born with post-traumatic stress, and with a high need to not be a burden to her mother or anyone else—which explained why she was so uncomfortable at getting special attention in class, and so determined to minimize her distress. She had a deep need to help her father, and by extension, everyone. The situation was a perfect storm for creating a codependent child. She pursued a degree in social work. However, "I started to attract energy-sucking people who knew they could manipulate me and I would take it. Until the regression class, I didn't know how codependent I was."

Deirdre took all three of my classes over a period of about four months. Her son was eighteen months old when she began the training, and by the third class she announced she was expecting a daughter. Because of the awareness she had gained from regressions to her own mother's womb, she was determined to find the help she needed to get healthy—physically, mentally, and emotionally—to provide an optimal pre-birth environment for her daughter. With the help of her doctors and her own hard work, when time approached for the birth of her second child, she felt better than she had ever felt. "There is so much peace in my world now by just putting myself first."

As she was going into labor she wrote to me, "*I get emotional as I write this because I am carrying a little girl in my own womb who is at the same stage of development as I was when my father was attacked. I can only hope that my daughter feels her mother's power now, and that she knows I am not depending on her for anything. My hope is that she feels my energy and will love herself the way I am loving myself at this point in my life."*

Prenatal trauma need not be as dramatic as Deirdre's to create problems for the infant. Remember, an unborn baby is reacting to everything going on in its world. When his mother experiences any trauma, the baby responds with an increased heart rate, and he may kick in protest. They can feel pain. During amniocentesis, the preborn will pull away from the incoming needle. The baby hears much more than you may realize; certainly raised voices, fights, jarring music, and loud noises all negatively affect the child. Bruce Lipton, in his lectures on conscious parenting, shows his audience a video of a woman undergoing a sonogram, while the parents are loudly arguing. "You can vividly see the fetus jump when the argument starts. The startled fetus arches its body and jumps up, as if it were on a trampoline when the argument is punctuated with the shattering of glass."

"An adult listening to conversations recorded through a miniature microphone placed in a womb," writes Dr. Deepak Chopra, "can understand over half of the words spoken by a man and over a third of the words spoken by a woman standing in front of the pregnant woman." A baby hears the mother's words more clearly—studies show that newborns recognize the sound of their mother's voice—because that sound comes not just from the outside but also through the body. If that sound is soothing or happy, the baby's brain responds positively.

We are not simply creatures whose lives are formed by our genetic inheritance, but rather by the environment in which those genes are influenced. That influence begins at the moment of conception. If you or your partner is pregnant or planning to be, please see the bibliography section for books that can help you create the best environment possible for your child's first vital experiences.

Chapter 2

"I Should Never Have Been Born": The Impact of Conception by Rape

> Working with a variety of techniques, such as hypnosis, drugs, and regressive psychotherapies, patients have reported on their earliest impressions, some going back—amazingly—to conception.

> Thomas R. Verny, MD,
> *Pre-Parenting: Nurturing Your Child from Conception*

Deirdre's trauma happened very close to the time of her birth. But just how early can an infant store memories? As Dr. Verny, who is considered the world's leading expert on the effects of prenatal environment on personality development, states in the opening quote—apparently right from the beginning.

It was 2:00 p.m. and time to meet my new client. At first I didn't see him in the waiting room. He had moved his chair closer to the potted plant and he couldn't be seen from my doorway. His face was hidden behind a magazine, and he didn't look up until I said, "Evan?" He was barely able to make eye contact with me as I greeted him. Fortunately, once I closed the door to my office behind us, he was able to relax enough to tell me why he was there. "I've felt scared my whole life, and down deep, I feel like maybe I should never have been born."

He believed he didn't deserve to be happy or loved, and his behavior was reflected in that belief. He had dropped out of college even though he had good grades, and for nine years had worked at what he called a dead-end job as floor manager of a chain store. It sounded like the two guys he called friends hung around because he was good for a loan or a free meal. But Evan was turning thirty and he wanted to change. Given he had at least symbolically hidden from me in the waiting area, I did not expect he would let me into his inner world right away. So I demonstrated what hypnosis was like by putting him in a light trance and coaching him as he created an inner safe place. We worked with a couple of "good" memories and he relaxed even more. I ended that first session with the post-hypnotic suggestion that his faith in this process would grow deeper and stronger.

During his second hypnotherapy session, I prompted him to go to his inner safe place, which he was able to do. In fact, he reported that there were a few changes in the place, "more light, and a big soft chair." That was a good sign. His subconscious mind had been at work, telling us something positive had happened between sessions. Encouraged, I directed him to go to the source of the belief that he shouldn't have been born. At first I thought I had overestimated how much he would be able to do in session two because he reported seeing "nothing." I asked him to use other senses: "Listen, feel, you may just know." He took a deep breath, and while he still couldn't see anything, he felt a lot. He felt squished, and upset, and he heard something . . . a rhythmic sound, like a heartbeat. "I think I'm inside my mother's womb," he whispered.

"Let's go with that and see what happens," I said. I asked him if he could tell how his mother felt about her pregnancy.

He looked startled. "She's ashamed. She shouldn't be pregnant; she didn't want this. She didn't want me!" He broke into tears and wept for several minutes. I put some tissues in his outstretched hand and asked if he was aware of his father. He said, "There's an angry man that comes around."

He frowned. "Wait, that's my grandfather. He's calling her a slut, a whore. He says 'I'll whip that bastard right out of you.' Now I'm really scared." Evan wept more, sad and afraid for his own life and his young mother who was only seventeen when he was born. What he hadn't known until he was an adult and had obtained a copy of his birth certificate was that his mother was single when he was born. He asked her about it and she told him that the man he knew as his father had married her when Evan was about eighteen months old. Even after learning his father had adopted him, Evan said he was too uncomfortable to ask his mother about his birth father.

At the third session, he decided he wanted to see if he could learn something about the birth father. Once in trance, I prompted him to recall his conception. Under hypnosis, he said, "I'm not seeing this but I have a strong feeling about it. I feel like a man my mother barely knew raped her. I sense violence, and I feel afraid."

We discussed whether it would be helpful to ask his mother about the man. He wanted to find out if what he believed happened, was true. But his mother was "pretty fragile and very religious," and he worried that it would upset her to talk about it. What he decided to do surprised me, but it turned out to be a good decision: he went to his grandfather. Because his grandfather had strong negative opinions about therapy and especially hypnosis, Evan said he was seeking help in finding his birth father for the purpose of getting his medical history. His grandfather told Evan that the "son of a bitch that knocked your mother up" was three years ahead of her in school. He had offered to give her a ride home after a football game and "took advantage of her in the backseat of his car." Evan said, "I asked him if it was a date rape but that term hadn't even been invented then." His grandfather supposed that it had been rape. He said that once she realized she was pregnant, she told her mother what had happened. Her mother told her to keep her shameful secret to herself, and "once she was showing, she was shipped off to some home for unwed mothers."

I groaned inwardly, recalling a similar situation with one of my friends from high school. I said, "She was blamed and made to feel ashamed."

"Very sad, and terribly unfair," Evan said. "I didn't tell Grandpa I knew he'd hit her. I just couldn't bring myself to say that."

Neither Evan's mother nor his adoptive father was an especially warm or affectionate parent, but they hadn't abused him. Most of his beliefs about his very existence came from his mother's shame—which he took on as his own; her wish that she wasn't pregnant—which he translated as she wished he didn't exist; and his grandfather's righteous rage, all of which occurred before his birth. Growing up, the grandfather treated him with disdain while doting on his two little sisters, which only reinforced his belief that he shouldn't be alive. After Evan got the truth from his grandfather, "the old man realized he'd blamed my mom for what happened to her, and blamed me too." Evan sobbed, "He asked me to forgive him. I couldn't believe it." That was the beginning of a big change in his family. A secret like this should be carefully revealed and it was. After Grandpa made amends to his mother, she eventually agreed to see a therapist. The therapist urged her to tell his married sisters, and when they learned the truth, they made a concerted effort to include Evan in their lives.

Evan claimed he could remember something that happened before his brain should have been developed enough to think with language. However, many regression therapists have reported cases such as this. One of the most important and classic texts on my bookshelf is a two-volume set: *Regression Therapy: A Handbook for Professionals*, edited by the late Winafred Blake Lucas, PhD. Volume II includes several chapters regarding prenatal events. Barbara Findeisen, MFCC (certified marriage and family therapist) contributed a chapter regarding destructive birth patterns. She wrote: "In beginning an exploration of the uterine state I use imagery to take the client back to just before conception.... This time is experienced as one of pure energy, of peace and calm joy. I then suggest that the client observe both parents and recount what awareness there is of each one. We then visualize the conception. It is amazing how often this can be recalled vividly." She related the case of a depressed and suicidal woman who was actively planning to take her own life. In regression she discovered her mother didn't want to be pregnant and was thinking about an abortion. The client believed she was responsible for her mother's upset condition and felt she should be dead. The insight resulted in a positive turn in the course of treatment.

Consider the work of Dr. Raymond Moody and many others who have investigated near-death reports. They are convinced that consciousness exists after death. If it exists after it leaves the body, we must consider that consciousness might exist prior to coming into a body. Of course, skeptics can claim it is all imagined, but I've had other clients who, after reporting conception or prenatal memories they had had no prior conscious knowledge of, checked the details with a parent or other family member and had their reports confirmed as accurate.

My heart went out to Evan. He was born believing his very existence created problems and pain for his mother. The family, not knowing anything about his erroneous beliefs, did nothing to correct those beliefs, and instead, reinforced them with benign neglect and outright rejection.

Evan responded well to inner child therapy. Because he was a kind and gentle man he was able to regard his infant-self with love and compassion. That compassion towards the infant translated quickly into compassion for himself. He was able to change his core beliefs to "I am wanted, I have value, and I'm open to being wanted by others." Self-love grew slowly, but deeply, and he stopped being afraid of people, especially loud-mouthed men. He treated that inner little boy like a son who deserved to be protected and loved. I knew things had permanently changed when he kicked the moochers out of his apartment and returned to school to get a business degree.

A person conceived by rape has a cellular memory of this violent beginning and will be affected by the mother's emotional turmoil during the pregnancy. It's my observation that the child takes it personally. An unwanted pregnancy might be interpreted as "she didn't want me."

"I was unwanted" too often becomes "nobody would want me."

Such was the case with another client, Marilyn, who had been adopted at birth by an older childless couple who doted on her. She was raised in an upper middle class neighborhood, given every opportunity to excel in school and socially, which she did, but she never felt "right." Certain her adopted parents had never shamed her, she still felt ashamed. She also had a violent temper, which reared its head when she felt slighted, or worse, abandoned.

Under hypnosis she regressed back to her conception. At first she reported a horrific blur of images: black formless creatures, blood, and weapons. I instructed her to move out a few feet from the experience and tell me what was happening. "A man is raping her (mother) at knife point. She's screaming in pain and fear." With tears streaming down her cheeks, she reported feeling scared, furious, and ashamed—unable to tell if they were her feelings or her mother's.

As I moved her forward through the gestation, I kept checking in with how she was feeling and what she was picking up in the environment. "Mother can't wait to get rid of me. All she wants is for this to be over. I feel like I'm drowning in her shame of having me." After her birth, when Marilyn was quickly removed from her mother, she thought, "She didn't want me. If my mother doesn't love me, who will?"

During the course of her work around this, she also revealed that she felt most sexually aroused via rape fantasies, and sought out partners willing to role-play that scenario. She had felt somewhat ashamed of what she called her kinky side, but less ashamed when she realized it was violent sex that had created her. She didn't keep in touch after the two sessions she had with me, so I don't know if her sexual desires changed or not. It was within her power to do so, however. I did feel that she was able to accept the replacement belief I suggested: "Even though I was not lovingly conceived, I love and accept myself. I am lovable and worthy of love."

Chapter 3

When Perinatal Trauma Created a Damsel in Distress

We can, for example, discover through direct experience that we had a breech birth, that a forceps was used during our delivery, or that we were born with the umbilical cord twisted around the neck. We can feel the anxiety, biological fury, physical pain, and suffocation associated with this terrifying event and even accurately recognize the type of anesthesia used when we were born.

Stanislay Grof, MD,
Healing Our Deepest Wounds

How do you explain a family in which one child is self-confident, ambitious, and dependable while another one lives from crisis to crisis, needing to be frequently bailed out of trouble? Thanks to the trailblazing work of psychiatrist Stanislav Grof, whose research regarding perinatal (the weeks before and after birth) trauma, and by others such as those affiliated with the Association for Prenatal and Perinatal Psychology and Health (APPPAH), we understand that our birth experience can set the tone for our style of being in the world.

In preparation for his birth, a baby struggles to move into position to begin his descent down the birth canal. It is a monumental task. To do that successfully takes effort and perseverance—and at the end, with help from mother's push, success! That infant begins his life with some sense that his destiny is in his own hands, and that he has the ability to succeed. He also knows that effort will pay off.

On the other hand, take an infant who doesn't successfully get into position, or who is in a womb that is too small, too tight—or a labor prolonged for any number of reasons. The mother may be anxious, but the infant is in crisis. He may start to panic, thinking he might die at any moment, and suddenly, a light appears and a hand reaches in and frees the baby from his terrifying tomb. Saved!

Children whose births were by emergency C-section surgery may re-create that dramatic beginning by getting themselves into one tight squeeze after another, always expecting to be rescued. Naturally, depending upon the environment into which a child is raised, these initial experiences will be reinforced, modified, or extinguished. If fearful children are overprotected and not encouraged to become independent, the pattern will only deepen. If children are taught early on to do for themselves those things they ought to be able to do according to their age, then that self-confidence and self-determination will grow and the child will transcend that traumatic beginning.

When I see a new client who reveals a history of getting into tight scrapes or crises, coupled with a need to be rescued, I always ask what they know about their birth. No matter what they have been told, I'll want to explore these earliest of experiences via regression hypnosis.

Such was the case of Valerie, a woman in her mid-thirties who initially came to me because of a cocaine addiction. She was in sales in a field that brought her into contact with wealthy entrepreneurs and high-profile celebrities. Valerie made a very good income, but much of it was going up her nose. She called herself a daddy's girl, and often asked her parents for money. It sounded like she lived from crisis to crisis, and somehow she always managed to find someone who would come to her rescue. But she was exhausted, scared, and ashamed not just because of the addiction, but for what she was willing to do to get the drug, such as having sex with men she didn't like or respect.

In hypnosis, when prompted to go to the source of her repetition of crisis and rescue, she reported re-experiencing the day of her birth—the long labor, the unborn child in great distress, feeling crushed and suffocating and panicky. She believed she was going to die. The unborn child couldn't move and then she stopped trying. An emergency C-section was performed, and suddenly—it was over. Her birth was the experience of crisis, hopelessness, and rescue. The intensity of the experience was imprinted in her body and mind and she compulsively re-created it.

Dr. Verny in his chapter "The Mystery and Power of Early Memory" wrote that intense and dramatic events become "flashbulb memories." Some memories are conscious—you would be hard pressed to find anyone who couldn't remember exactly where they were when they got news of the 9/11 attacks, or a baby boomer when they learned of President Kennedy's assassination. But, intense memories are frequently repressed and therefore unconscious. He observes: "Behavioral reenactment of early trauma continues even if the context has changed." He told of a woman who, as an infant with a congenital closure of the esophagus, was fed via a feeding tube while lying flat on her back. As a child she fed her dolls in that position, and as a mother, she fed her infants the same way, having no conscious memory of how she herself was fed.

He quoted obstetrician David B. Cheek who asked patients while undergoing hypnosis to recall their births: "After checking his records, he found that a hundred percent remembered the way their head rotated as it came out of the birth canal. Almost everyone remembered which arm came out first as well.'" He also quoted David B. Chamberlain, a leader in the field of prenatal and perinatal psychology. He studied mother-offspring pairs who separately under hypnosis "recalled startlingly similar details of the offspring's birth."

Valerie had accessed her traumatic birth memories, and as a result she was able to understand the concept of *repetition compulsion*. She saw how she had unconsciously gotten herself into difficult situations and then looked for someone to help her out. She also understood the connection between the excited *high* of cocaine and the high of her dramatic birth. After a session or two of being mad at herself, which was a necessary part of her recovery, she vowed to make changes. First, she had to stop medicating herself with cocaine and alcohol. A motivated client, she agreed to enter a residential treatment program, followed by Narcotics Anonymous meetings. She got clean and sober first try, which actually surprised me given her childhood pattern of giving up when things got tough. (At least, she didn't relapse during the two years she was my client, and that made for an excellent prognosis.)

When she returned to me for aftercare hypnotherapy, we started with inner child work. Like my student Deirdre and my client Evan, Valerie had to learn to love and care for her infant-self. I asked her to imagine that someone had just left a tiny baby on her doorstep and now she had to take responsibility for meeting the needs of the child instead of looking to others. She learned to use positive language when talking to herself, and in working the twelve steps of Narcotics Anonymous she practiced patience and persistence. She also responded well to Progression Therapy, which is a process of helping the client envision a near future after her issues are resolved. Valerie saw herself in the future, independent and addiction free, and in a relationship with a partner who was an equal, instead of that knight in shining armor of the past. Once she could see this, it became her new vision of herself. With the new vision, she was able to change her playmates and playgrounds.

Resolving symptoms that originate perinatally

I mentioned at the beginning of this chapter that the manner of one's birth can set the tone for how one deals with the world. It can also result in pathological beliefs about oneself.

Guilt. A number of clients with chronic feelings of guilt, especially when interacting with their mothers, discovered the source of that guilt was their experience of mother's labor pains. In one case, because his mother was a screamer, the horrified baby adopted the belief that he was responsible for his mother's "extreme" suffering. Unfortunately, in relating the story of his birth, his mother often made the statement that he'd hurt her. As a little boy, he took that statement literally and put on the mantle of "bad child"—a spirit-killing mistaken belief. There's nothing he could do to change that belief because there was nothing specific to work with. If a parent says you are a bad boy for hitting your sister, you know what you did, and what you can do to become a good boy. But being the cause of suffering? How good would he have to be to become acceptable? An impossible feat. Once the source of guilt was found, and he was able to see the experience from his adult perspective, he let go of the guilt.

A client suffered from guilt because her mother died giving birth to her. I facilitated a conversation between her and the spirit of her mother. In cases such as hers, sometimes this is an imagined encounter, but sometimes the client reports an actual presence. This can be a very moving conversation. It often begins with the adult child apologizing, and always ends with the mother protesting the guilt and telling him or her to let the guilt go. This freedom from guilt allows the client to finally and fully grieve the mother's death.

Shame. The most likely reason anyone is born feeling ashamed is when his or her mother was shamed by others or felt internally ashamed of the pregnancy. Or if the first few months of life were fraught with shaming words about natural things like poopy diapers or crying. Along with inner child work, homework includes visiting a newborn and considering whether this precious little being is to be held accountable for their circumstances or reactions to their environment.

Loud Noises. One client said he had been anxious his entire life, and the worst of it was around loud noises, especially the sound of arguments. He'd been raised by his mother, whom he described as sweet and gentle, so he was surprised when he found the source of his fear was from fights between his parents prior to his birth and during the first few months of his life. His mother had hidden his birth father's verbal abuse of her and the reason she had left him.

In hypnosis, I had him recall the fighting between his parents. I then suggested he step out of the womb and watch the fight until it was over. Up until then he'd only remembered the noise and fear, which replayed in his mind in a loop. I said, "You now see that your parents made a lot of noise when they fought. Was anyone in danger?" He thought so at the time, but what he realized is that no one was in danger now. Noise isn't itself dangerous unless at very high decibels, and rarely signals true danger. I ended the session with having him tap away the residual emotional and body memory with a technique developed by Gary Craig called The Emotional Freedom Technique, or Tapping. (See appendix for more information.)

Claustrophobia. The fear of enclosed places that was created during a complicated birth can be healed or reduced with a guided visualization of an easy birth, followed by imagining themselves as a child running free in a large open space. Homework involves actually walking fast or running in a park or field. If the claustrophobia persists in spite of trying the above, more regression work is needed. There is more about that in the chapter on phobias.

Fear of death. While I have uncovered a number of sources of the fear of death, one apropos to this chapter is that which was created when a fetus felt threatened, either by a potential miscarriage, learning his or her mother was considering an abortion or attempted an abortion, or by complications before or during birth. My usual treatment for this type of fear of death is a re-birthing. (See appendix for more information.)

Giving up. Part of the healing process for any kind of birth trauma, including a C-section, includes visualization of a positive gestation and a successful self-birth. I have clients imagine putting forth a great deal of effort to come into the world on their own. I then give them the post-hypnotic suggestion that "today or very soon you will have confidence in yourself, great determination and pride in being in charge of your own life, and you will drop all need to create crises, and to be rescued." To fully change their way of being, they must mindfully put forth effort—physical effort such as regular exercise; mental effort such as taking a class and finishing it or meditating; and emotional effort such as managing powerful feelings.

Obsessions. Certain fears or obsessions that seem bizarre may have originated during a traumatic birth. I worked on the psychiatric wing of a small town hospital my second and third years out of graduate school, and before I had the skills to investigate issues by going to their source. I'd love the opportunity to go back and work with those psychotic people who were tormented with visions of blood, feces, or genitalia; obsessed by pain (sadistic or masochistic); or by symbols or visions of the crucified Christ, or Satan. I fully expect that at least some of those visions would have been sourced to pre-birth or birth trauma. Those are among the themes described by Dr. Stanislav Grof in his thirty-plus years of research.

Today, with a private practice, I don't have access to such patients. I doubt that any Western hospital is brave enough for regression therapists yet, but perhaps given what is coming to light in the area of birth psychology, the next generation of therapists will have that chance.

As biologist Bruce Lipton pointed out, "The subconscious works only in the 'now.' Consequently, programmed misperceptions in our subconscious mind are not 'monitored' and will habitually engage us in inappropriate and limiting behaviors." Through cell research Lipton determined that genes and DNA do not control our biology ... our beliefs do. When therapy works, it is because the therapist has assisted the clients to correct their limiting or negative beliefs about themselves and how the world works.

Chapter 4

Adoption and How an Unwanted Baby Became a Gentle, Loving Mother

In humans, stressful life events during pregnancy obviously include unwanted pregnancies and unwanted babies.... And what about anxiety? ....In addition to the now recognized trauma of child physical, sexual, and emotional abuse, I propose to add the trauma of the separation of a child from its mother. It is difficult to change our thinking about adoption from that of a wonderful, altruistic event to that of a traumatic, terrifying experience for the child. It is difficult, and understandably so, for the adoptive parents to look at the infant and think that he might be suffering. Yet how can he not be? Except in the case of some truly enlightened adoptive mothers, there is no acknowledgement of the child's loss of the original mother. Therefore, there is no permission, either implicit or explicit, to mourn.

Nancy Newton Verrier,
The Primal Wound: Understanding the Adopted Child

Imagine a conscious little being growing in the womb of an untreated mentally ill seventeen-year-old girl. Imagine how she feels, believing she is the cause of her mother's illness or of hearing repeatedly, "I don't want you, I can't keep you." Then imagine that after her birth she is in a group foster home for six weeks before she hears the words from her adoptive parents, "you are home now." If you can imagine that, then you will understand how Gina was born scared, insecure, and overly sensitive to any messages from others that she was unwanted or unworthy.

Deciding to see a therapist is a big decision. Often people are desperate when they call me especially when it comes to dealing with addiction. Usually they are desperate because they have tried other options or alternatives that haven't worked, and now their lives are unmanageable. Gina wanted to stop drinking. Her husband was getting fed up and her kids were showing signs of stress. It was getting hard to hide her drinking from colleagues, and she knew her job performance as a counselor in a large private school was slipping. She had tried hypnosis with another practitioner and it had worked for a couple of months, but now she couldn't stay sober for more than a week or so at a time. She also struggled with obsessive thinking especially about what other people might think about her.

In her first session, I prompted her to go to the source of the craving to drink. "I just don't want to feel. To feel that pit in my stomach. It's always there. I worry about everything. Am I doing a good enough job at work? Am I making the right recommendations for the students I work with? Do the teachers respect me? Are those interns I supervise learning anything? Are my kids okay? Does my husband still love me?"

When prompted to go to the major cause of her worrying thoughts, she went back to the womb. "I feel utterly alone." Gina wept, "She's scared (the mother). She keeps saying, *I don't want you; I can't keep you*. It makes me feel scared. What's going to happen to me? Who will take care of me?" And then she uttered the words I often hear from adoptees: "What's wrong with me?" It is such an error in thinking to believe the reason a woman relinquishes an infant for adoption is because there is something wrong with the baby. It is a common belief among adoptees, however. Even with those who were adopted by caring and competent people.

The Needs of the Infant

The desire to know where they came from, to know who their birth mother is and why she relinquished them looms large in the psyche of adoptees. It's an existential question we all grapple with: *Who am I? Why was I born?* And most importantly, *Do I matter?* We all require a sense of belonging and connection and all of that is being addressed during the first nine months of life—in utero. A child developing within the womb of a healthy woman who wants the child and is willing and capable of nurturing him or her, is getting the messages: *I am precious, I am wanted, I matter, I belong to her and in her world.*

In his groundbreaking book from 1981, *The Secret Life of the Unborn*, Dr. Thomas Verny speaks of intrauterine bonding. He referenced a study by Dr. Stirnimann, "which showed that months before birth, mother and child were already beginning to mesh their rhythms and responses to each other," which explains why a newborn so quickly bonds with his mother. Or not, in Gina's case.

Verny gave an extraordinary example of the lack of pre-birth bonding, which he'd heard from his friend, Dr. Peter Fedor-Greybergh, one of Europe's leading obstetricians. It was of a newborn girl who turned her head away from her mother when the breast was initially offered to her, the opposite of what newborns do naturally. They discovered she would drink heartily from a bottle, so there was nothing wrong with her appetite; she just would not nurse. In an experiment, they asked another mother to nurse her, and she readily accepted her breast. Dr. Febor-Greyberg asked the birth mother if she had any idea why her child would turn from her and she seemed to have none. Finally he asked, "Well, did you want to get pregnant then?" The mother answered, "No, I didn't, I wanted an abortion. My husband wanted the child. That's why I had her." Dr. Verny wrote: "[The infant] had been painfully aware of her mother's rejection for a long time. She refused to bond with her mother after birth because her mother had refused to bond with her before it."

I asked Gina if she knew anything about her birth mother. She told me that as an adult, when her state opened adoption records, she made contact with her birth mother. "That turned out to be a big mistake. She started calling me, asking for help, for money. She even showed up at my workplace. It was obvious she had an untreated mental illness. Finally I had to get a restraining order against her."

With what she had learned about her birth mother, and what she had uncovered in her regression to the womb, we worked with the emotions and beliefs of that infant. Because of her training in psychology, Gina knew what to say to her infant self, and her caring, heartfelt sweetness towards her felt genuine. She told her inner child, "Our mother is mentally ill. She was too sick to think of you, too sick to take care of you. You had nothing to do with her illness. She didn't want to be pregnant, but it wasn't about you. She didn't know you at all. You are safe, you are wanted, you are good enough."

At the next session, she said she had been feeling much less anxious and managed to not drink all week. However, just the day before this session, something happened at work that threw her into an emotional tailspin. "Someone from the executive office blamed me for a mistake someone else made. Our boss called me into the office and started going over our code of ethics, like I'd committed a crime. I was humiliated. I hadn't done anything wrong." She was teetering on the brink of resigning.

Oh, how we hate being wrongly accused, and those who already have a fragile sense of self-worth can be devastated by it. Today what Gina needed was help in standing tall while things got sorted out at work. Sometimes, in regression work, the answer to a problem is not in finding the source, but the way through. As Gina went into a deeper state, and envisioned going down stairs, they turned into stairs in a castle. She found herself in the body of the court jester—she had spontaneously regressed into a past life.

"I serve the king. I juggle, tumble, do magic tricks, and I can say things to the king that no one else can get away with, because I do it with funny songs." The jester enjoyed a long and fulfilled life. He married a woman "full of mirth" and who "loved to laugh." He not only cheered people up, he consoled the sad and dying with special songs. Upon his death, we called upon the jester to help Gina deal with her problem at work.

Gina laughed out loud. "He sings a wicked lyric about the woman who caused the problem, and then said to me, "Don't let the mean people get you down. Don't suffer the fool. Fool the suffering." She left the office with a smile and a spring in her step.

Like the wisdom of the book, *Don't Sweat the Small Stuff*, the jester helped her take the panic out of the equation, and reduced her fear of the woman who caused the problem so that she was able to take the facts back to her boss, and clear her name. She decided to call upon the jester frequently so she could lighten up.

As Christmas grew near, Gina's adopted mother, who lived hundreds of miles away, became very ill. Gina felt like she should be by her mother's side, taking care of her, but she couldn't take time from work, or leave her own family. She felt guilty and disloyal. In hypnosis, she returned to an earlier Christmas.

"We're in our first house. I'm only two or three years old. Mommy is very sad. She's in the kitchen, sitting at the table, her head in her hands." Her daddy was passed out drunk on the living room floor, by the Christmas tree. "I feel very alone, and I go into the kitchen and crawl up into my mother's lap to be held." Adult Gina could see that her mother didn't respond to her.

"Christmas is sad. Mother left him on another Christmas. Dad was getting violent, and his drinking was worse." Gina's mother took her and her brother away in the middle of the night, and they fled to her mother's home a few states away. "Daddy was threatening to kill her and himself." Gina sighed. "Mother deserves to feel safe."

"And so do you," I said. I reflected on this child who was adopted into a violent home, and who by the time her mother got the courage to escape the violence had stopped thinking about her own needs. But why did she feel disloyal because she wasn't hurrying to her mother's bedside?

"I took care of her a lot. All during high school she was ill, fatigued. I shopped, cooked, did the laundry. I was always worried about her health."

Suddenly she put her hand to her mouth. "Julia, I just remembered something. I was in the second grade and Mom got pneumonia. I stayed with the people next door. You know, she never let me forget that I didn't take care of her."

"Second grade?" I said. "You were seven years old." Enough said. Gina came out of that memory and declared, "That was outrageous. It wasn't my job to take care of her. I needed to be taken care of, and good thing the neighbors were there for me. The jester just showed up and he says I should get her [the inner seven-year-old] something to make her happy."

"What are you going to get her?" I asked.

"A puppy."

In that moment she realized she had felt responsible for her adoptive mother's wellbeing from the very beginning instead of the other way around.

It was easy to understand how that could have happened. You'll recall in chapter one, I talked about what journalist Annie Murphy Paul called "biological postcards from the world outside," answering questions critical to the baby's survival. "Will it be safe and protected, or will it face constant dangers and threats? Will it live a long, fruitful life, or a short, harried one?"

The postcards Gina got said she would not be safe or protected. Nine months of worry about that mother's ability and capacity to take care of her plus a belief that she was the cause of her mother's suffering resulted in the subconscious decision—*I will do everything I can to make her feel safe and happy so then she will take care of me. My survival depends upon that.* At birth, she was immediately separated from that mother, and for six weeks she was motherless.

Nancy Verrier, quoted at the beginning of this chapter, is an adoption specialist. She calls the severing of the connection between the child and her birthmother a *primal wound*, "which affects the adoptee's sense of self and often manifests in a sense of loss, basic mistrust, anxiety and depression, emotional and/or behavioral problems, and difficulties in relationships with significant others."

When a dysfunctional couple adopted Gina, nothing happened that would change her view of the outside world. She simply transferred her survival tactics to the new mother.

I encouraged her to say, "I didn't create or cause what happened to my adoptive mother, and I can't fix it." She let go of the guilt of not dropping everything to take care of her mother. However, when she was able to take time off from work a few weeks later to visit, she was pleased to report that she felt more compassion towards her mother because of the absence of guilt and feeling of obligation.

Over the next few weeks, we worked with her wounded inner children and her limiting beliefs, and things were going very well regarding her mood and self-esteem, but she still struggled with intermittent drinking binges. The post-hypnotic suggestions to not drink were not taking root. We talked about a residential treatment program and two weeks later, she made the decision to enter treatment. It was a program geared towards high-functioning professionals, and she did very well. One of the most important gains in treatment was not taking things personally ... a simple concept, but very hard to do. That reduced her stress at work considerably.

At seven months of sobriety, we both realized that she had made a huge shift in her way of viewing herself and her world. In a trance state, she found herself immersed in the imagery of a huge water-filled cavern, well lit and beautiful. In the center there was an island. "From this island, I'm exploring the depths and I'm finding treasure."

"If you think of the symbols as representing yourself, what does it mean?"

"I'm shifting perspective from what's wrong with me to what is right." Gina had her eyes closed. If they had been open she would have seen me throw my arms in the air and my lips silently shout "Hooray."

"What else is on the island?"

" A tree, well set, with pictures of my children hanging from the tree."

"And the message ...?"

"I'm a good mom. I'm doing okay. I've had so many doubts about doing okay, but now I'm seeing rays of light coming into the place, shining a light on what has been hidden."

A few more sessions and she was ready to graduate from therapy. That precious child who came unwelcomed into the world through a frightened seventeen-year-old, and who was then raised in a house with an immature and needy mother, and a violent, alcoholic father, had learned to love herself, trust herself, overcome addiction, and become a gentle and loving mother to her own children.

See appendix for resources for adoptees and for those who adopt.

Chapter 5

Womb Twin Survivors

> Vanishing twin syndrome has been diagnosed more frequently since the use of ultrasonography in early pregnancy. A conservative estimate of frequency is that vanishing twin syndrome occurs in 21–30 percent of multi-fetal pregnancies.
>
> www.AmericanPregnancy.org

There are some people who seem to have been born, not just scared but in deep grief and feeling empty or guilty for simply existing. As adults they cannot understand or explain why. And there are people who seem desperate to find their other half. They often channel this desperation into seeking the perfect mate, but their need to hold their partner tight often results in complaints of suffocation or engulfment and they find themselves back in the worst possible situation they can imagine—being left and alone.

Marta, a colleague of mine, had the symptoms of the first scenario. She had plenty of reasons to feel miserable. She was the middle daughter of a classic narcissistic mother, the "off with their heads" kind. The author of *Understanding the Borderline Mother,* therapist Christine Lawson, would classify her mother as a Queen type, with a strong "Witch" side, threatening to strike without warning. "Queen" Maxine gave each daughter a name beginning with M, because as is typical of self-absorbed parents, her children were mere extensions of herself. As was also typical, she projected different qualities onto the girls: the eldest was the perfect one, Marta was the bad one, and the youngest was the lost child. Born with a heart defect, Marta also had other health challenges, like gallstones at the age of thirteen, requiring surgery.

"I had bouts of being suicidal. Once in a restaurant, I think I was in junior high, I decided to confess to my mother I wanted to kill myself. What she said was, 'What's wrong with you? There's nothing in your life that would warrant that. Shame on you.'"

By her forties, she'd hit rock bottom. "I went into the woods with a water glass. I broke it and used a jagged shard to cut my wrist. I tried twice, but somehow I couldn't make it work. I remember being aware that there was not a conscious thought to stop myself. It was more like a silent, yet gentle presence that halted time for a moment so that I couldn't follow through. In an altered state of some kind, I dropped the piece of glass and began walking out of the woods." She never had another suicidal thought even though she continued to suffer.

Along with three bouts of severe depression and feeling stupid and worthless, she had crying jags she could not explain. "Three or four times a month, for as long I could remember, I'd collapse into feelings of utter grief, as if someone I deeply cared about had died. I'd hear myself saying, *I'm sorry. I'm so, so sorry.* As I got older, I'd wonder what mistake I'd made to feel so bereft and guilt-ridden."

With suicide no longer an option, she entered into therapy. In the process she gained strength and insight. "I realized I was fed up with Mother's guilt trips and shaming, and I cut off all contact. Then I began to heal."

After many years of therapy and personal growth work, discovering she was intelligent (intelligent enough to earn a PhD in psychology), and surrounding herself with kind people, the depression lifted, her self-esteem grew, and for the first time in her life she began to express herself and feel joy. Still, the crying jags persisted.

Her career as a professor of early childhood development led her to several of the leaders in the emerging field of birth psychology. She attended a week-long intensive workshop with affiliates from The Birth Psychology association and she began to look at her own birth trauma. She and her therapists made connections between her heart problems and her insecure attachment to her mother, Maxine.

"Then when I began talking about those episodes of grief, I suddenly felt myself in the womb, and things began to make sense."

Marta's voice got very quiet, dreamy-like as she recalled what happened.

"It's early, sometime in the first trimester, and I'm looking at my twin brother. He doesn't even have the look of a fetus yet, but I know he's male. His name is Andrew." She burst into tears. "And he is starting to die. I'm watching him die. He is ... slowly ... disintegrating. No! We were going to face this together."

She described a physical sense of utter grief, similar to what she had felt at the death of her first beloved pet, and yet she kept saying she was sorry.

"So, Marta," I asked, "instead of feeling anger towards him for more or less bailing, as many womb twins do, you felt sad, but also guilty. Any idea why?"

"I felt guilty because I was still alive ... and he was dead. I felt guilty because I was there and watched him slowly leave and I couldn't do anything about it. I couldn't help him live. Many times in my life I have felt that I would have been happier if I had died with him. I felt sad because I would be left to live alone without my twin. There was and still is a void where he should be. I joke sometimes that he was the lucky one; he didn't have to live a life with Maxine as his mother in this incarnation. I think that it would have been very hard for him. She wouldn't have been emotionally able to care for two babies at one time. It was probably a good thing he had second thoughts about his future life and chose to make an early exit. I don't hold it against him. I love him and always will. I realize it sounds strange to say this about someone I only knew so briefly, but decided I needed to make contact with [the spirit of] Andrew."

She discovered she was able to make that contact on her own. "My brother said to me, 'I want you to not be so sad,' and I said to him, 'I don't know how to live without you. You are supposed to be in my life.' The grief was our connection. That was not healthy. We needed to create a different connection. So, we decided to meet together on a train from time to time. When I'd feel that deep longing, I'd quiet myself, go inside and go to the train. He appears as an adult. I see his shoes; he's dressed up. I sit facing him, on the seat across from him. We don't talk, we just meld. After a while, maybe two minutes, he leaves, and I get off the train. I'm ready to go on. I used to have three or four of those crying jags per month, throughout my whole life. Now they are rare."

One day her therapist asked her if she was aware of the time of day when the grief would wash over her, and she realized it was around 3:30 in the afternoon. "That's when it happened. That's when he began to die."

"Fifty-eight years of not wanting to be here, and now I do. I laugh now, joke now, I love to laugh. My husband says I'm so much more peaceful and at one with myself these days."

The number of pregnancies that begin as multiples is estimated to be about one in eight. But often within a few days or weeks, the stronger one prevails and the weaker one ceases to grow. The tissue may be reabsorbed, or flattened from the pressure of the survivor and visible upon birth. This is called "vanishing twin syndrome." There is some danger to the surviving fetus and the mother should this death occur after the first trimester. The twin birth rate in the United States is slightly above 32 twin live births per 1,000 live births. Althea Hayton, a writer and public speaker from England and the person who first coined the phrase "womb twin survivors," wrote: "Statistical analysis of various studies of twin pregnancies has revealed an astonishing statistic: for every twin or multiple birth, six womb twin survivors are born."

A little research into mainstream medicine regarding vanishing twins revealed no mention of the psychological effects of this loss, as far as I could find. However, it appears to me that Hayton is correct, the memory of sharing the space lingers, and if a twin survived long enough for the two bodies to be physically entwined, that intimacy is sorely missed.

Another survivor is a friend of mine whom I'll call Dorothy. We met in a writing group many years ago. She said, "From a very young age I had this feeling I was missing something. I couldn't articulate it then, but as an adult looking back I'd say it was indescribable loneliness." After years of struggle and searching, she found the answer in 2008. She missed her twin brother. A twin who had died in the womb.

Dorothy was a wanted and much cherished child. After eighteen years of failing to get pregnant, her mother finally chose artificial insemination. A shy, traditional woman, she underwent this procedure without her husband ever knowing about it. My friend only learned the truth from her mother after her father died.

"When I was very little, she'd find me sitting on the floor behind the couch, crying, and all I could say was, 'I want a baby brother.' I know it broke her heart to see me so unconsolable. The only wish I ever made when I blew out my birthday candles or wished upon a star was for a baby brother."

She obsessed about babies and especially multiples. When she saw a baby or a pregnant woman, the response she felt was "as great as the feeling I got later when I was pregnant with my own children or as powerful as falling in love."

I asked Dorothy when she first thought she might be a womb twin survivor. She laughed. "I'd written a poem and was surprised by the words that came to me." She titled it "Duplicate Soul." She hasn't been able to find the poem but snatches of it came to her: "liquid fluidity/ floating in something/ a thin and gossamer veil/ my sadness in looking for my duplicate soul." The last line was "and I was left alone, searching for a duplicate soul."

She didn't think she'd heard the phrase "duplicate soul" anywhere else, and didn't understand the poem. She did an Internet search on duplicate soul. That led her to twins, which led her to lost twin. Then she found Althea Hayton's website about womb twin survivors. (www.wombtwin.com) As she read the symptom list and stories from other readers, she heard herself say, "Oh, yeah. I just knew." Dorothy didn't relate to all the symptoms, not even to a lot of them, but of the ones she did, "They explained everything."

The "dream of the womb" is how Althea Hayton refers to the womb memory. She says during her four years of research she discovered that "survivors spend their life constantly re-enacting their dream of the womb. Nothing is more important to them than that." I wondered what Dorothy's dreams of the womb were. What behaviors had she re-enacted?

"If I made a friend, I would feel very close to her, close and important. I'd get hurt if she wasn't as close back. If she pushed me away, or even slighted me, I would think she was cruel. I'd say to myself, I'd never leave her. I thought we were put on earth to find our other half. No, more than that, I thought we were *meant* to find our other half." She wanted a brother but filled the longing with girlfriends. She thinks it was because boys didn't get close in the manner she needed.

She felt scared and vulnerable when away from home. "I worried that I wouldn't be found." At eight years of age she was hospitalized and when she was moved to a different room, she panicked at the thought her mother wouldn't be able to find her. Riding the school bus she worried she might never get home again. When she was five or six, she went to stay with her aunt but was taken home in the middle of the night because Dorothy wouldn't stop crying. She went away to camp when she was eight, but "I was almost ill with homesickness. The camp nurse came to visit me. She was kind and caring. The big deal here was she had figured out I needed being cared for. I'd fall in love with anyone who did that."

Friends of mine have twins, a boy and a girl. I saw an ultrasound of them taken at about six months. The twins were entwined and each was touching the other's face. It was precious. They are now almost eleven, and sadly the boy has Asperger's Syndrome, and while he's very high functioning, as is typical, he relates differently to people, including his twin sister. She clearly longs for that remembered intimacy and I've seen her scream at him in frustration.

One of my clients, in her early forties, is an identical twin. She describes her sister as detached and critical and she refuses to have the close relationship my client desperately longs for. Even though married, my client feels a deep loneliness that she feels only her sister could fill. My point is those twins bonded in the womb, and that loss of intimacy is devastating.

Dorothy felt that same frustration and loneliness. She just didn't know who she was missing.

"What things did it explain when you finally figured it out?" I asked Dorothy.

"Why I have difficulty having more than one friend at a time. I need to give all my attention to one person. It explained why I was always looking for my soul mate, and why even good relationships were not enough to fill the need. I feel great empathy when others are sad. I feel sorry and in great pain when I see animals treated with cruelty and neglect. I can't go to the animal shelter." Her favorite make-believe game was nurse. "All of my dolls had red spots on them. I probably smothered partners, but some were like me. We'd joke about how we were both co-dependent. I wanted to not just be close but intertwined, and I'd hang on long after the other person was done."

Finding the source of her anxiety, sadness, and clinging personality was a great relief. Knowing where the sadness came from, "that it was a loss, enabled me to grieve, and grieving brought me to the other side. I feel good and confident now."

She consulted with a woman who reads the Akashic Records (claimed to be the records of the soul). "I asked her about my twin brother, and she said he was a watcher. He had been watching me for years. At night I used to hear my name being called. I'd wake up and answer 'what?' When I was little I thought it was God, now I think it was him. His spirit stayed attached to me after my birth."

I wondered if some of the fears of being lost, scared when away from home, and of mother not being able to find her, were actually his fears. She decided perhaps they were. "I couldn't separate his feelings from mine."

"Is he still attached?" I asked.

She looked at me for a long while and then grinned. "No, I believe he left about six months ago. No wonder I'm no longer anxious."

Advice for parents of a womb twin survivor

If you know your child is a survivor, and has emotional or mood problems such as anxiety or depression, there are things you can do to help. Wait for the right time: when they say something that makes you think they are remembering their twin, and it might show up as an "imaginary playmate," or when they are six years old or older. Tell them the truth in a way they can understand, being careful not to make them feel responsible for their twin's demise. For instance, don't say, "You were the strong one, the one who survived." Rather explain something along these lines, but that fits with your own beliefs: "Lots of times two babies start to grow in a mommy, and they are called twins. But sometimes one of the babies changes his or her mind about being born and goes back to heaven to wait for another time or another mother. Their tiny little body just disappears. That happened to your twin. You might remember it, but maybe you don't."

Then invite them to tell you what they think, and answer their questions. Of course, if your twins were both born and then one died after birth, the survivor will most certainly have memories of their brother or sister in some fashion. In either case, it might be appropriate to create a ritual to help the child say goodbye to the twin. It was the process of grieving the loss of her brother that turned things around for Dorothy. For Marta it was making contact with Andrew, and knowing she still could if she needed it. A child you will meet in chapter six, whose twin sister died six weeks after their birth, decided to place a little marker in her memory in the garden where family pets are laid to rest. Another child, once he learned about his lost twin sister, cried himself to sleep for a few nights. He also began to understand why he clung to friends and family so tightly. After a few days, he bounced back and was able to let go of many of his clinging ways.

If the symptoms or mourning continue more than a few days, consider seeking professional help for your child.

Chapter 6

The Brave Girl: A Micro-Preemie Who Survived All Odds

Being born too soon is widely recognized as a traumatic beginning. Regrettably, this is a rising problem: one in thirteen babies in this country are now born prematurely … [and] … prematurely born brains are traumatized brains, which puts babies at risk of adverse health and mental health outcomes. For NICU babies, the combined stress of being isolated from the mother and the daily pain and discomfort of a NICU unit leads to what Dr. Heidelise Als of Harvard Medical Schools calls "neurotoxic brain-altering events"—in other words, trauma.

Robin Karr-Morse, LPC, with Meredith S. Wiley, JD,
Scared Sick: The Role of Childhood Trauma in Adult Disease

We've looked at the traumatizing effects of conception by rape, of being an unwanted baby, of a complicated and dangerous birth, of losing a twin before birth, and of being present in utero during an external traumatic event. There's an additional trauma that doesn't get the attention it should, and that is the trauma of a premature birth.

Kayla, whom I've known since childhood, is the adopted daughter of my friend, Donna and her partner Randee, and had multiple challenges before and soon after she was born. The birth parents were both drug addicts. The father was uninterested in a long-term relationship or being a father to Kayla and her identical twin. He wanted the mother to have an abortion. The birth mother refused the abortion and agreed to adoption.

At just 28 weeks gestation, she went into labor due to preeclampsia, and the twins were delivered by C-section, each weighing just 1.7 pounds. They had the usual feeding and breathing issues of micro-preemies: too small to suckle, too weak to breathe on their own. Sadly, Kayla's sister died at six weeks due to an infection. Because the birth mother had relinquished them at birth, there was no one there to mourn that death, and no mother to visit Kayla during her extended hospital stay, except of course the hospital staff, and perhaps some volunteers.

After nine weeks in the neonatal intensive care unit of the hospital, Kayla's birth mother and father chose Donna and Randee to raise Kayla. The tiny infant finally heard the words, "Mommie is here."

Donna described the Neonatal Intensive Care Unit (NICU) as chaotic with "beeping machines, crying babies, bright and flashing lights." What a lonely, confusing, stressful, and pain-filled way to start out life. Birth psychologists believe that preemies feel pain more acutely than full-term babies, so even those little heel sticks for blood work must have upset her greatly.

"We were with her in the hospital every day for a week," said Donna. "She responded very well to hugging, singing, and cuddling, and at the end of that week, we got to bring her home."

During those first few weeks, it was necessary to monitor her for apnea and to make sure her body temperature did not drop below normal. So she wore a tiny little cap and warm sleepers and a blanket at all times. When her body temperature did drop, one of her mothers held her skin-to-skin until she warmed up. She was eating two ounces of formula about every two hours (along with breast milk provided by a lactating mother). She was held or carried in a front pack at all times except for nighttime when she slept alone in her crib. She responded beautifully to being held and touched and was for the most part a relaxed, calm baby.

Even though they live in another state, I've been able to watch Kayla's progress and challenges since she was brought home from the hospital. She thrived surprisingly well; however, she did not crawl but rather scooted across the floor with one leg somewhat forward, and she walked late, at eighteen months.

By the age of three, Kayla was becoming more anxious, reacting "in fear to beeping noises and flashing lights." By the age of seven, the fear had developed into a phobia. Donna said, "She'd been so excited to attend her best friend's birthday party, but when we arrived at the roller-skating rink, she took one step inside the building, saw the flashing lights, and froze. She would not go farther. She started crying "*I don't wanna go in!*" Even when her friend came over, she still would not budge. She could not physically step into that room with the flashing lights and loud music. Kayla handed over the birthday present at the door and we left."

About a month later she tried to attend another birthday party, this time at a bowling alley—but unfortunately there were more flashing lights and loud music. Again, she froze at that door. "I just can't do it," she said. She handed the present to her friend at the door and again they left.

Beginning therapy

Greatly concerned about her growing phobia, her parents sought help from a therapist who worked with children with birth issues. "The therapist related this to the ten weeks in the NICU and used Eye Movement Desensitization and Reprocessing (EMDR) with good success." (See appendix for more information about EMDR.) After four EMDR sessions, Kayla was taken back to the same roller-skating rink for a walk-through—and she ended up putting skates on and actually going out onto the floor to skate in the spotlight.

Evaluation and diagnosis

By fourth grade, a neuropsychology evaluation identified problems with working memory, processing speeds, executive function, and attention. She was diagnosed with anxiety and dyscalculia (difficulty with math, and time issues) and given an Individualized Education Program (IEP) for math and executive function. She also exhibited some of the behaviors of Attention Deficit Disorder.

Fortunately, Kayla had fabulous support at school and an understanding teacher, school nurse, and principal, and a few good friends. Her biggest struggles were in math and class participation. Struggles erupted every night over homework. Kayla would shut down and freeze when confronted with work she saw as too hard, especially a whole page of math problems. Lots of tears, tantrums, and frustrated parents.

"Julia, Kayla had a panic attack last night," Donna said over the phone. "It started with her heart pounding, then she was sweating and shaking uncontrollably." She said it took about an hour to help Kayla calm down and finally fall asleep.

Once a person has experienced a panic attack, they worry about having another. While not in themselves dangerous, the attacks are very frightening, and the unfortunate victim will start taking measures to prevent it happening again. Kayla became more inner focused. Her teachers noted her inability to concentrate and focus on her work and, with encouragement from their doctor, her parents agreed to put her on Concerta, a medication used to control symptoms of lack of attention and/or hyperactivity. "The drug seemed to help her focus, but it also made her more anxious, nervous, and emotional."

At the end of the school year, and with some of the pressure off, they decided to take their planned vacation to Mexico. Kayla did well with the flight and seemed to enjoy the resort, especially swimming with the dolphins. However, on the final day of their vacation, they went to visit the site of an ancient ruin. "It was a very hot day and the heat was oppressive as we walked through the jungle. Kayla started to feel faint and uncomfortable, and then began to panic: racing heart, sweating, faint-headed, shaky legs, and then uncontrolled shaking all over. Her head hurt too. We rushed back to the resort and worked at getting her cooled off. It took several hours."

That was rough on everybody. A panic attack at home is bad enough, but in a foreign country? Just getting her on the return flight home was hard. Closed spaces can be a problem. She was extremely anxious throughout the day and the following day back at home. "We did three things right away. Got her into a counselor for trauma work, took her to a specialist for relaxation exercises, and took her off of Concerta, the ADD medication. She seemed to improve somewhat, but a month later she had another panic attack.

The Flood

The floodgates had opened. It looked like every issue she could have had as a result of her rough beginning had thrust through her subconscious mind and multiplied ten fold.

- She worried about things she had heretofore taken in stride, and refused to participate in extracurricular activities like girls' choir. She often refused to leave the house, and she became fearful of movie theaters.
- She began to question her identity. She became more obsessed with needing to know if her birth mother cared about her. At times she pushed Donna and her partner away, exclaiming they weren't her real parents, and she didn't belong with them, while at the same time feared being without them.
- She wept over the loss of her twin sister, and was rather inconsolable at her lack of siblings and being with the "right family."
- She started restricting her food out of a fear of choking. She refused to eat anything solid.
- She worried about getting contaminated by food, nail polish, or poisoned by toxic gas coming into her room.
- She was tested for low blood sugar, but tests came out negative. However, the doctor recommended she eat something every two hours.

Unfortunately, Kayla then became obsessed with eating constantly—mostly protein bars and Ensure drinks. She had to have food in her pockets at all time.

- She avoided getting over-heated, and could not bear wearing outer clothing in a room of normal temperature.

Where could they turn for help? What symptoms should they tackle first? Should she be hospitalized? Should they try more medication?

Donna asked me for advice. There is a shocking lack of help for children, even in metropolitan cities, and I was at a disadvantage because I wasn't familiar with what was available near her. She had tried to get help, but after dozens of phone calls, a two-month wait for a psychiatric consultation, a health insurance plan that didn't cover the only available hospital for children, and cognitive therapy that seemed to make things worse, Donna was stressed out, discouraged, and frightened.

I had three pieces of advice. "Even though you are worried about her, it is important you stay calm and tell her there are solutions for every problem and that you have faith in her." That was important, because frightened children will fall into despair if they sense their parents are also frightened. If they feel you are worried about them, that adds to their worry.

I urged her to stop trying to talk Kayla out of worry by appealing to reason, but rather to say that there is nothing dangerous going on except her brain was sending bad messages to her right now—and she would help her change that.

The third piece of advice was to read the section about medicating children in Robert Whitaker's book, *Anatomy of an Epidemic*. Even though she had stopped the ADD medication on a hunch it was making things worse, I wanted her to have the facts about ADHD medications based upon an NIMH-funded investigation which extended over seven years and concluded: "Medication use was 'associated with worse hyperactivity-impulsivity and oppositional defiant disorder symptoms' and with greater overall functional impairment." Whitaker is an award-winning medical journalist and what he says about medicating children should be intuitively obvious: We should not medicate a still-developing brain. He wrote: "The medicating of children and youth became commonplace only a short time ago, and already it has put millions onto a path of lifelong illness."

I wanted Donna to be armed with the facts because I knew that desperate parents will often acquiesce under pressure to medicate their children. It might seem unreasonable to start with what she shouldn't do, but she understood that I just wanted to be sure she didn't get talked into doing something that would make matters worse. She read the book, and decided she would continue to seek alternative solutions.

Divine intervention

Then we talked about options. I recommended she consider taking Kayla to a naturopath to check her hormones because of the hot flashes (at age ten she was already developing breasts), and to investigate the food issues. Then a wonderful synchronicity happened which turned things around rather quickly. I believe that miracles happen when you have taken steps to help yourself. Donna called it "divine intervention." When searching for a naturopath, she found one who also offered neurofeedback. As she read the information on neurofeedback—the indications for its use and how it helps—she had a gut feeling this would be helpful. And she was right. In just a few weeks of treatment, Donna wrote to me:

"This has been by far the most successful treatment in her process. The feedback started training her brain to self-regulate better. It interrupted her trauma patterns and helped create tranquil and more effective brain patterns."

Kayla's anxiety was greatly reduced and her eating returned to almost normal. She was more able to focus on homework and complete tasks. The naturopath also discovered she's gluten intolerant and getting gluten out of the diet ended the stomachaches and "wooshy" feelings. That news made me wonder how much the food Kayla had eaten at the Mexican resort had contributed to the panic attack there.

Family ties and identity

As significant as the body and mind work was, equally important was the work of her heart and spirit. Donna realized that at the core, Kayla needed to understand her relationships—why did her mother give her away, did she think of her, did she matter to her? Donna sought out the birth mother to see if she would be willing to tell Kayla she mattered. It was a risky business. You never know what you'll get when you contact a birth mother, especially one with a history of drug abuse and unstable relationships.

Donna said, "We were beginning to see all these disconnected issues going on in Kayla's life as connected. Here was a kid trying to work out her adoption issues—some pretty heavy existential stuff. Her life was not making sense to her, and it felt out of control. It was as if the traumas associated with her conception, her premature birth, her difficult delivery, the loss of her twin, the absence of her mother, and her ten weeks in the NICU caught up with her. She did not feel safe in this world nor did she feel like she was where she was supposed to be."

Kayla's birth mother was located through Facebook. And on hearing the news that her birth mother wanted her to know 'that I think about you every day,' she burst into heaving sobs. A dam of emotions broke loose. After several delays and excuses by the birth mother, Kayla finally met her and her seventeen-year-old half sister. She was elated after the meeting and began to fantasize about going to live with them. Later that evening, Kayla threw a tantrum and declared, "You aren't my parents; I don't have to mind you!"

But instead of a positive ongoing relationship, the birth mother's erratic life made it difficult for her to stay in contact. "The challenges with eating came after weeks of no contact that followed that first meeting. Kayla finally admitted she was afraid that they didn't like her because they hadn't made contact again. After some prodding, she revealed a fantasy she had of an idealized birth mother, one who was probably in great pain over missing her child.

Donna persisted and after several e-mails, another meeting was scheduled. They went to a dog park and walked their dogs. Her birth mother made all sorts of plans and promises—none of which ever materialized. Two things happened after that day. Kayla finally understood how troubled her birth mother actually was, and that she was far better off at home with her two moms. And, Donna caught a bit of news she stored away for later: her birth mother had given birth to another daughter four years earlier who had been taken from her. Donna made a note of the child's name, Ellie, and of her adoptive parents.

Even though Kayla had been warmly welcomed into both sides of her adoptive family and has had a supportive circle of families of her classmates and friends, she clearly yearned for a connection to her biological family. Through Facebook sleuthing, Donna also found Ellie's family. She made contact with the adoptive parents and after some friendly phone conversations, the families got together.

Donna sends out updates to all the adults who care about Kayla, and I was thrilled to get this e-mail about meeting Ellie:

"We all hit if off right away. Turns out there's a boy, also adopted, who is closer in age to Kayla, and they spent the evening laughing, running, playing DSi games, and kind of falling in sibling love. We all fell in love with Ellie."

After about four months of get-togethers, Kayla had a very positive relationship with "her little sister" and her "brother" (although there's no biological connection). She said it doesn't take the place of her birth mother but she is happy.

During a recent visit to their home, Kayla, who had recently turned eleven, showed me a school project— her very complicated family tree. In the tree roots, she included her birth mother, grandmother, and her two half sisters. In the arms of the tree are her adoptive parents and their parents and grandparents. Beside her own name, she included her deceased twin sister. Donna told me they had conducted a little memorial service for her when she was processing grief and loss with the therapist.

Blae and Multi-Moldi

Kayla now began an exploration of her feelings. Until now she had difficulty naming her feelings and talking about her fears. What she did was fascinating. "She gave names and colors to her feelings. First she drew a feeling, gave it a name, and then described the feeling. "Blae" was a wild purple scribble and named for all the fears and feelings combined—everything, including her evil menace she had named "Multi-Moldi." She then made them into characters in stories which involved the happy, strong characters taking care of the scared and angry characters. So far she has named and drawn twelve feelings," said Donna. This is an important part of treatment for kids who worry. It's called "name it to tame it."

From surviving to thriving—hard work paid off

I have the utmost respect for Donna and Randee for their dedication to finding solutions for Kayla, who was clearly in desperate trouble. At times they were understandably frightened and overwhelmed, not knowing what to do. While Donna's partner is a mental health counselor, Donna is not but she had a very valuable skill: she listened to her daughter—how she felt, what she feared, and what she needed.

"Mostly we held a safe place for her to express all her fears, doubts, hopes, and thoughts. We understood this was her journey and we were there every step to walk through it with her. It wasn't about us." Ten-year-olds can tackle big issues, and that is what she and her moms did together.

As we collaborated on this chapter, Donna wrote:

This past week while at Lake Roosevelt with her friend [name removed] and her family, without hesitation she rode and drove a 4-wheeler, rode and drove a wave-runner, rode in a very bouncy inner tube behind the wave runner, and climbed up steep sand dunes. She liked it fast, bumpy, and steep! This is not Kayla of one year ago. In fact, she also joined three summer camps and had no anxiety issues—nothing but fun and the excitement of learning and making new friends.... Looking back at the past year, it is hard to remember all the pain and difficult emotions we went through. Looking forward we see a resilient budding preteen who is more able to roll with the punches, more compassionate towards others, less volatile, more able to laugh at herself, less fearful, bright-eyed, physically strong, excited about trying new things, adventuresome, and just plain engaged in her life. She is joyful, loving, interesting, funny, and looking forward the future.

(See appendix for books and resources regarding adoption.)

Chapter 7

Separation Anxiety: The Boy Who Clung to His Mother

The parents of James Leininger were first puzzled and then disturbed when their two-year-old son began screaming out chilling phrases during recurrent nightmares, such as, "Plane on fire! Little man can't get out!" … [After extensive research they] were drawn inescapably to a shocking conclusion: that James was reliving the life of James Huston, a World War II fighter pilot who was killed in the battle for Iwo Jima—*over sixty years ago!*

Bruce and Anne Leininger,
Soul Survivor: The Reincarnation of a World War II Fighter Pilot

In the summer of 2009 I received this e-mail: *"My son [Danny] is seven years old and has spoken with me about one of his past lives which ended tragically during WWII. He suffers from tremendous separation anxiety, may have a tendency toward OCD, has some diagnosed sensory-processing issues and a fear of water (he died on a ship that sunk). We have gotten some professional help for his sensory issues and tried counseling for the anxiety (didn't work). I cannot help but think that if we can get him regressed so that he can have some closure with his previous life that he will hopefully be more grounded in this one."*

I'm always touched when a parent takes their child's report of a possible past life seriously, particularly when they are reporting a traumatic end, as did the parents of James Leininger, described in their book, *Soul Survivor*. The fears a child expresses give us clues as to what will likely be core issues they may struggle with their entire life, if not resolved in childhood.

I also have great sympathy for any parent of a child with separation anxiety. It is an almost impossible task to know when to be stern and when to sympathize as your little one is screaming, "Don't leave me!"

When Jenny called to make an appointment, I learned more about her son's separation anxiety. It had gotten so bad that he would not go to school without her being in his classroom. It was difficult for him when she left the classroom, even for a quick trip to the office. (She was there under the guise of being the teacher's assistant, which I'm sure was very welcomed by the teacher.) While she seemed happy enough to help the teacher out, she admitted she really wanted her own life back.

Danny is very likable—a sweet face with a touch of mischief in his eyes, and more talkative and open than many children. He was very observant, too. He saw things in my office most adults don't notice, like the chambered nautilus fossil and large celestite crystal on my side table. He found my treatment chair fun because it swivels.

He told me about the past life during World War II that his mother mentioned, adding his name and several other details, and "I also remember being in the Civil War … on the good side." He was willing to undergo a regression to see if we could find a way for him to be less worried about being away from Mom. I explained that a past-life regression was much like the way you remember things you did yesterday. "You are relaxed in the chair, and you and I are talking, but you will see pictures in your mind, and hear your own thoughts, as you go to other lifetimes."

Danny was a good regression subject, as most children are, in that he visualized and knew what was going on without questioning it in the telling. He easily returned to the memory of being in a submarine, of it being torpedoed, and then of his sudden death. He reported this without emotion, which is also typical. Before processing that death, I asked if he thought there were other past lives that were adding to his being scared, especially around losing a loved one. He said *yes*.

His process was interesting and suggested he had access to the gestalt of the experience—he didn't relive the lifetimes, but rather summarized them. One was in ancient Egypt. He said he was a man who made paper, and during a famine his five-year-old son died; the next was in modern times, he was a male, a geologist who died on Mt. St. Helens during the volcanic eruption of 1980; then he immediately reported a death during an explosion in a New York subway. He said it was "driver error." His last thoughts were of his mother who was waiting for him at the platform. Then he said, "There's one about a cemetery in New Jersey, but I don't want to know." He opened his eyes and that was that.

I asked him to imagine a peaceful and safe place and he chose a beach in Hawaii. I prompted him to gather up all the fear and sadness from the past lives and then to let it all just disappear "because you see and you know that right now you are 100 percent safe."

Jenny reported later that as they left my office he walked ahead of her instead of holding her hand. He crossed the street on his own and then told her, "I'm okay now." When they got back to the schoolyard, he ran off to play with his friends. She said, "I was flabbergasted. He was grounded and peaceful." Naturally, his mother and I hoped this confidence would last, but it didn't. Still that didn't mean it wasn't useful. He now knew how it felt to feel okay, and she knew he could do it. Their beliefs were changing.

We continued to meet. I made him a relaxation tape, which he listened to on his own (pretty remarkable for a child) and taught him to think of worry as a "bully." He came up with a physical description of the worry bully, and then we figured out creative ways to get rid of him. Danny imagined himself larger than the bully, and saw himself able to kick it very far, like over the moon or all the way to China. Danny took to that process, and another one called the *worry hill*, with his mother's gentle reminders. (See appendix for books for helping anxious children.)

Pre-birth contribution to anxiety

Jenny had some difficulty when she was pregnant with Danny. "At three months, I started spotting. As I was driving to the doctor's office, I kept saying, 'hang on. I'll take care of you.'" During the final two months, she was on bed rest, and had some fears of losing him. She wondered if he had picked up her worries. It seemed connected.

Perhaps his past-life traumas were stimulated in the womb? What likely triggered the recent increased anxiety happened earlier in the year when she'd been very ill for much of two months. Mother and son had a powerful connection. I suggested she do some regression work herself to see if she could help shake loose their mutual fears of losing each other.

Mother's past-life connections to Danny

The first past-life Jenny reported likely took place in the nineteenth century. Her name was Elizabeth, and she seemed to be a gentle person who loved painting the flowers that grew in her garden. She married John at the age of eighteen, and they soon had a daughter. Sad to say, Elizabeth had a weak heart. "It hurts all the time, and holds me back." She couldn't have more children, but she more or less "took in" a three-year-old boy, William. Her own daughter was headstrong and harder to love than William. "He found a place with us. He feels safe here. His own people weren't any good."

Elizabeth died young, a short while after William married and moved away. I asked about the last time she had seen him. "I went to his home. They, his wife and two children, were poor but happy." After her death, I asked Jenny if Elizabeth had any regrets and she said, "I wanted to do more for William." Her husband had drawn a line regarding just how much they would help William, but she had wanted to help much more than they did. She realized that Danny, her son today, was William then. "They both have big hearts."

The next regression began with a premonition. "I'm seeing a train tunnel. It's cold and damp, and smells bad. I'm waiting for a train and my stomach hurts. Something bad happens on the train." I wondered, of course, if she was recalling the same past life that her son had previously reported, and it turned out she was. She got many details. Again, she was a woman, married to an insurance salesman in the 1940s, "a good man." She had two children, a boy named George (who was present-life Danny) and a girl who was several years younger. While she loved her family, she was bored at being a housewife. She was a college graduate and longed to be a professor.

She described the fateful day. "I'm on the platform, waiting to pick up George after attending a baseball game. He's fourteen. I hear a terrible sound, and there's a weird wind. The train doesn't come. Finally, I go back up to the street and see my husband with a policeman. (She sobs.) They tell me there was a crash, and George was killed. We bury him in the cemetery on the hill."

George's death hit her hard. Even after two years, she remained depressed and numb. "I need to show up for my daughter but I don't want to. I feel guilty, she's a good girl, but I can't let go. I miss George. My husband and I just walk around each other." She died at an old age, and she was ready. Her last thoughts were of George, "I wish I could have known him as an adult."

Had George, after his death, stayed around his family? Was he aware of how much pain his death had caused his mother? His last thoughts at his death had been of her waiting at the platform.

Jenny carried over strong emotional connections to Danny from her past lives: regret at not helping William have a better life, and unresolved bereavement at the loss of George. Those feelings were likely stimulated when she feared she would lose Danny (again) even before he was born. It seems that his attachment issues were inevitable.

Things were slowly improving, but he was still not able to go to school without her being there, and he still was shifting decision-making and problem solving to his mother. I asked if they would consider a rewards program. Danny said he would be willing to work on more independence and we discussed his incentives. He would earn points for not questioning his mother when she said she was leaving the classroom for a while, points for not checking up on her, and points for solving a problem on his own. He also could earn points for going outside to play on his own.

At the next session, he was eager to share his success in terms of points earned (which is one of the reasons behavior modification works. It shifted his focus from controlling Mother to controlling himself). Within six weeks he had full days at school without Jenny being there at all. His *worry hill* was smaller, and he practiced kicking the worry bully away. He was taking car rides with people other than family members; his school went camping and he stayed in a tent without a parent. He was proud and Jenny had her life back. The coolest thing at that appointment was when he said he wanted his mother to go to the waiting area while he underwent hypnosis. It felt like graduation day for Danny.

This is not to say that my work with him and his mother alone cured Danny. I was part of their team. They also had family therapy, and Danny had occupational therapy and was tested for food sensitivities, of which there were several, and more recently—Brain Gym, a program described in this book's appendix.

In following up some eighteen months from his last appointment with me, Jenny said Danny continued to do well. "He still has some anxiety and wants reassurance he will be picked up after school. He still doesn't like separation but has done great with a babysitter." He continues to work with an occupational therapist on sensory and coping skills and attends a social skills class with boys his age.

Danny is lucky to have parents who put the time and effort into helping him overcome his learning disabilities and anxiety. He's a bright and curious boy, but he would likely not do well as an adult had his problems been left unaddressed. One rarely outgrows anxiety, and I don't think anyone truly outgrows separation anxiety either.

Adult separation anxiety

This fifty-year-old client's stated goal for therapy was to "get over my ex-husband." Vera had been divorced for three years, he had remarried, and yet she thought of him "all the time." She was highly dependent upon him. In addition to alimony, she often asked him for extra financial help, and frequently called him for advice, moral support, or when she was afraid. She was extremely anxious and could not be alone. Vera managed to find people to stay with her—her adult sons, a son's girlfriend, friends, and neighbors. She had a job, but after several months off due to anxiety, which had been triggered by illness, she was about to lose the job. She was retreating from the world, and hiding at home.

A friend drove her to sessions, and a couple of times we had to do work over the phone. Her stated goal (getting over her ex-husband) was a starting place, but she clearly had separation anxiety. We had to peel off the layers. The initial regression work addressed the precise fear of being alone when ill, and that took her to a memory of being in the hospital for a tonsillectomy when she was seven years old. "I'm supposed to be asleep but I went into a tunnel. I'm very scared and I feel all alone. I'm looking around and there's nobody there to take care of me."

Reports of "going into a tunnel" are suggestive of either a near-death experience (which seemed unlikely with such minor surgery), or of dissociation. I presumed it was the latter—a part of her consciousness separated from her body, not uncommon in those who suffer from high anxiety, especially children. It's a form of protection. A way for the child to escape the unpleasant reality of a situation, when he or she can't physically leave. It can result in disorientation when the child does come back. Sadly, when Vera returned to her body and woke up, she was in an empty room—there was no one there to help her get oriented. That made her feel even more afraid and abandoned.

Vera wept. "My mother left me alone a lot. Soon after my tonsils were out, she took my two brothers and sister on a trip and left me with a neighbor. I hate being alone."

"Is there an earlier experience that made this feel even scarier?"

"Yes," she reported, still in the hypnotic trance. "Now I'm in my mother's womb. She's scared, and I'm scared. I'm stuck in there. I'm waiting a long time. I need someone to help me, to get me out of this!" Finally, like the client from chapter three, a C-section was performed and she was rescued—that classic set-up for re-creating stressful situations, and then crying out for rescue.

"Is there an experience earlier than this one? Look into your soul's history."

She reported finding herself in a garden, a woman in black. "I'm in mourning. I just had another miscarriage. I've only given birth to one son, but I've lost several babies. My husband is indifferent to me. He has a mistress. I don't like him either." She identified the husband from the past-life as her present ex-husband. "He did it to me again," she sighed.

She dies young, from another miscarriage, her sole surviving child only twelve years old. (sobbing) "I can't bear to leave him."

This was her pattern—early loss and abandonment, problems with leaving and being left. No wonder she was suffering, and no wonder this fear felt so deeply ingrained in her. She had much healing to do.

She created a healing place in her mind's eye and brought her inner girls—her preborn, infant, four- and seven-year-old selves, her wife and mother selves, and the woman in the garden from her past life. She did a beautiful job of telling each of them they were not alone, and that she would take care of them. She understood the importance of staying in the present and strengthening the bonds within herself.

Fortunately, over the next few months, along with counseling, she also started working with a naturopath who diagnosed and treated a serious thyroid condition. But more, he expected her to get well and encouraged her to take on more responsibility for her own recovery. It helped that she developed a crush on him, which allowed her to fantasize about her future instead of living in the past. Fortunately, the doctor had good boundaries, and the crush remained only a crush. That doctor gave her wings. This relationship was a steppingstone for her: from dependence to positive transference (the naturally occurring feelings of affection and attachment a patient develops in a healthy doctor/patient relationship) to independence. I was glad he was on her team. His work with her was complementary to mine.

Thyroid issues can increase anxiety, akin to turning up the volume on one's worries, or in some cases even causing it. Once that was treated, her anxiety was greatly diminished, and the shifts and insights she had in therapy took hold. She was now able to work on other issues: procrastination, fear of flying, and avoidance. Because she was now inner focused and no longer looking outside herself for help and strength, she easily discovered the sources of those issues and their remedies.

At our final session, she reported she had successfully flown by herself to a foreign country and back without anxiety, and she was growing her own business—something she'd not been able to dream of three years earlier. Vera proved that with work, one can overcome separation anxiety and abandonment fears. "I'm a very different person in my fifties—no longer is that fearful little girl in charge!"

Chapter 8

Night Terrors: The Scary Man at the Window and Other Children's Fears

> For many children, the fear may look irrational because the triggers are not apparent, but if parents would listen to their children and ask thoughtful questions about their fear, they might learn something about what underlies their anxiety. To tell a child their fears are just their imagination is unhelpful, discouraging, and dismissive of what might really be going on.
>
> Julia Ingram, MA,
> "How Mainstream Psychology Is Missing the Mark"

Parents can feel quite helpless when their child awakens at night screaming in terror. They desperately want to understand, "where is that fear coming from?" But their child rarely can put his or her fear into words without help.

This couple had accommodated to their son's night terrors, which started around age five, to the extent that by the age of ten, most nights he was sleeping on a cot at the foot of their bed. Every night, with encouraging words, his mother would tuck Douglas into his own bed, and each night he would promise to try to stay there. After a few stories, a drink of water, a discussion of whether to leave the light on or off, his door open or shut, and pleading tears for Mom to stay a little longer, his exhausted mother would finally leave his room. Every night she hoped he could make it through the night. Once in a while he would. But most nights by the time the adults were in bed, he was there at the door pleading to sleep in their room. He rarely had full-blown terror episodes at this age, but the anticipation of future episodes kept them all on edge.

Anyone who has watched the nanny-type programs on television may shake their heads and say the parents had reinforced that infantile behavior and what they should have done was made him stay in his room until he'd learned the art of self-soothing. That occurred to me too, until I met Douglas. His wasn't the typical waking-up-in terror sleep problem, at least not anymore. He was terrified to go to sleep, and his terror began as he was nodding off. In his case, he could put it into words. "I see this scary man's face looking in the window, and I just know that as soon as I'm asleep, he's going to come through the window and kill me," he said. While this could have been some kind of imaginary monster, the family wondered about a ghost or spirit.

His mother described occasions when Douglas reported seeing things other people didn't see and had reported some premonitions about people that later came true. He talked about seeing Indians who lived in the woods near their rural home and then he laughed and said he was the only one who could see them. His mother hastened to add that the land all around them had been home to Amerindians two hundred years ago. Obviously, all of his claims fell within her metaphysical belief system. The previous year, he had been evaluated by a child psychologist who wondered about psychosis, but his parents thought that was extreme and not related to the context in which he saw things. I certainly took note, however.

Douglas was a gifted child creatively, but challenged by severe learning disabilities, and had a hard time with school. Furthermore, being sensitive and anxious, he was the target of bullies. Together we had to figure out whether his so-called clairvoyance was real or an unconscious defense against facing his fears and emotional challenges. Either way, we needed to find a way to make him feel safe, self-sufficient, and in control of his emotions.

His mother had found me on the Internet after reading Carol Bowman's book, *Children's Past Lives*. As a toddler, Douglas had mentioned his "other family" and his "other mother" occasionally. The initial appointment had been made for a past-life regression for her son, and after listening to his story, and impressed by his intelligence and motivation, I felt that could be a useful place to start.

Because he found his own room a scary place, I suggested we start there. He was agreeable to hypnosis and easily went into trance. The regression revealed the story of a little girl between four and five years old by the name of Hannah. "Mom is in the kitchen making an omelette." Douglas was able to see the whole story as he described what happened next. "The house is on fire. I run upstairs. Mother can't find me and runs to the neighbors to call the fire department. The window cracks open (in Hannah's room) and a strange man starts to come into my room (a fireman). I didn't know him so I run into my closet and hide. I suffocate to death. Now I'm scared of the dark and men at windows." This from a boy of ten.

I was impressed with the way he put it together. Out of trance he said, "I did just the opposite to try to save my life. I should have run outside, but instead I hid upstairs where I couldn't be found until it was too late. My poor mother."

The regression was somewhat helpful. He shifted away from fear and into sympathy for little Hannah. He talked to her from time to time, until he was ready to say goodbye to her. The fear of the man at the window lessened too. But he still couldn't make it through the night in his own bed.

Several more regressions revealed his core issues: fear of death and of hurting his mother. Traumatic deaths showed up in eleven past-life reports, the ones causing him the most difficulty now being those in which he was murdered, buried alive, drowned on the Titanic, and died in his sleep (unaware he was dead). Chapters nine and ten, regarding agoraphobia, detail the problems that occur when one dies unaware. His concern for his mother showed up in one past life in which they were husband and wife and he was killed in a carriage accident. His last thoughts were of concern for her welfare. That concern showed up even before Douglas was born.

Pre-birth anxiety

As I increasingly saw how much Douglas identified with his mother and how her worries became his, I suggested we explore his pre-birth experience. His mother had told me he was born asleep. I wondered how any infant could sleep through his own birth. (It wasn't a C-section either.) I did a quick search on the Internet and found that being *born asleep* was generally used to soften the reality of a death prior to birth, but I found a few cases of infants born asleep who survived just fine. Rare, but not unheard of.

As I prompted him to remember being in the womb, he said he knew his mother was sick. "I feel worried about her. I hope she's okay. I hope I'm not the one who is making her sick. I hope she likes me. I think she won't like me (because he assumes he's making her sick?) so I'll will have to be extra good." As he reported his birth he said, "I feel bad for her, for the birth struggles." As I noted in chapter one, having concern for your parent even prior to birth is the perfect setup for co-dependency.

I learned from his mother that she had been very ill, and that she was told she should not try to have another child after him (he had an older brother). Had he picked up on that? She had wanted to have a daughter, too. Interestingly, after doing very well for months, he'd had a relapse. We realized it was around the time of his birthday.

As for his being born asleep, it may have been a coping behavior that started in the womb—to check out under stress. I observed him doing that on many occasions.

Another behavior that started in the womb was scanning for what Mom was doing and feeling. It turned out that part of the reason he had a hard time staying in his own room at night was that he was listening for evidence his mother was still there, and all right.

Treatment goals and results

The primary goal was to get Douglas sleeping in his own bed all through the night. Secondary goals were overcoming his phobias, extending his comfort zone, staying focused (not spacing out), and increasing his confidence and self-esteem.

It took a combination of approaches to achieve the first goal. He learned self-hypnosis to calm himself in bed and to say "no" or "I reject this thought" when having scary thoughts. He had to repeat to himself, "I don't need to know what Mom's doing," and to say "no" when he found himself listening for downstairs activity. He had to remind himself that the man at the window was from another time and place, and had nothing to do with "now." His family had to stay firm and stick with a rewards program (earned after five nights in a row of remaining in his own bed).

They were very excited one day to report that his fear of bridges was gone. In fact, all of his phobias were greatly reduced or gone after the regressions. He was placed on a low dose of Prozac for a few weeks by his family doctor, and enhanced with 5-HTP and occasionally St. John's wart and melatonin for sleep.

The family felt certain there were spirits in the house, and they took steps to clear them out by smudging (burning small bunches of cedar and spreading the smoke throughout the house). I was told it seemed to help.

His self-esteem gradually improved with a focus on his interest in art, and particularly puppetry and animation. A technique I like to use to give people hope for their future and something to look forward to is a progression; that is, looking forward to a potential present-life future, or a future lifetime. It is most helpful when someone is stuck in present circumstances and can't imagine their life being any different. The other thing I wanted to accomplish with Douglas was to have him see himself getting older. In many ways his behavior, even as he was going on twelve years old by then, was of a younger child and it was time for him to start thinking like his age.

I can't control a progression. I can only suggest future movement, and the rest is up to the brilliance of my client's high-wise self—and this was brilliant. He reported seeing himself in a future lifetime, a man in his thirties, a resident of a South American country in which he was an artist working for an animation studio, "one of six animators." He saw himself getting married to a woman from work, moving to a big house, having children. "Our boy is five years old. He draws with me."

This vision of a future self was exciting to him, and gave wings to his career aspirations. Portland has several animators and professional puppeteers, and he was given tours of studios, advice, and training on making puppets. When I saw him last, he proudly reported he was doing puppet shows for "little kids," his anxiety was minimal, he was off the Prozac, sleeping in his own bed, and making it through the night. His own spiritual beliefs were helpful, in that he felt the love and care of his guides, and he called upon them for help. He is likely quite clairvoyant, and time will tell if that becomes a problem again, a useful gift, or if it goes away.

Babies remember too

Early in my discovery of past-life regression, I formed a study group by putting a notice in our weekly alternative paper. The core group that responded to that ad met regularly for a few years and several of them played a part in the creation of my second book, *The Lost Sisterhood*. One of the most psychic of the group (her past-life name in that book was Anarisa) had a baby girl during the time we met regularly. She shared this story:

"It was in the middle of the night. I ran to the room and the baby was standing up in her crib, pointing at the floor and screaming in terror. I looked down and I could see what she was seeing—dozens of snakes writhing on the floor. I immediately knew that she was reliving a prior lifetime's trauma." She picked up her child and told her she could make the snakes go away with the wave of her hand. She showed the baby what to do, and she did it. That was the end of night terrors for that child. She empowered the child to make the scary thing go away. That's what matters.

Many inexplicable behaviors of children may have their roots in pre-birth or past-life experiences. Take these examples:

- A ten-year-old child from an affluent family would hide, hoard, and sneak food. In a regression session, we found two things: 1) Her mother hadn't wanted to gain a lot of weight during her pregnancy and dieted on low-fat food and diet drinks. In reporting her experience in the womb the girl said, "I feel hungry all the time. I want more and she won't give it to me." 2) A past-life in an orphanage with "too many children and not enough food." She died of starvation at a young age. She didn't know her age, but her mother said, "I'll bet it was six, because that's when all of this started."

- A six-year-old boy was afraid of dogs, even tiny ones, to the point that he finally refused to be outdoors at all. He would run from the family car into the house, or school, or the shopping mall, until he saw a woman with a seeing-eye dog there, and that was the end of shopping. When prompted to go to the source of the fear, he first recalled a memory from the previous year in which a neighbor's dog jumped on him and knocked him over. Since most kids would get over that, I said, "See if there are any other stories in your mind about scary dogs," and he said, "that time I was a man and I was sick and a whole bunch of dogs started biting me, and hurting me and killing me." After that discovery, he quickly overcame the phobia.

- A nine year-old-girl who was allergic to bananas. When I asked her to find the story of why, she reported being a child who sailed in a big ship across an ocean, and all she had to eat was bananas. "The little green ones made my lips hurt, but the squishy ones made my tummy hurt, and the black ones made me throw up. The ship made me sick too, and I'd throw up and then my mother would make me eat another banana."

As I said in the introduction. I believe there's an explanation for everything if you just ask the right questions.

Chapter 9

Agoraphobia: When an LSD Trip Ripped Open Buried Memories

The phobia of streets and open spaces (agoraphobia)—the counterpart to claustrophobia—the connection with biological birth is based on the contrast between the subjective sensation of enclosure and constriction and the ensuing enormous extension of space and experiential expansion. Agoraphobia is thus related to the very end of the birth process and emerging into the world. LSD subjects reliving this moment in the psychedelic sessions characteristically describe a deep fear of impending catastrophe and annihilation associated with this final transition.

Stanislav Grof, MD,
Beyond the Brain: Birth, Death and Transcendence in Psychotherapy

One of the most debilitating and baffling of anxiety disorders is agoraphobia, most commonly thought of as a morbid fear of open spaces or of being caught alone in some public place. Trapped in its extreme throes, the victim is unable to leave home at all. Most sufferers have a small range in which they are able to travel, like to work or school if not too far, but they have little or no social life, except when people visit them. Getting help is next to impossible. Even if the best practitioner in the country is two miles from their home, if that office is outside of their comfort zone, they can't get there.

The disorder starts with a panic attack. One panic attack often leads to more, and soon the fear of having another one leads the desperate sufferer to find ways to avoid one by any means. It is much more complicated than just trying to stave off an attack. My clients talk about the altered state they find themselves in. "I feel like I'm just going to fall off the earth, or fly off into space." Another said, "I feel like I leave my body, and the terror is, I might not come back." Many can't be alone because they fear being in a situation where there's no one to help them if they are in crisis. It is hard to put into words, and impossible to explain to others how it feels. Those with the disorder often feel frustrated and angry when people say they know how it feels because they've felt panicky themselves, and like that old book title, they recommend *you should just feel the fear and do it anyway.* "It's like my friends think I'm just not brave enough, or trying hard enough. They just don't get it."

Olivia was able to see me because my Tucson office was within her travel zone. She sought my help because her best friend was getting married in six months and wanted her to be the maid of honor. The wedding would be in Phoenix, which was just a two-hour drive, but to Olivia it may as well have been halfway around the world. She was highly motivated to beat this problem.

It had been a few years since her last panic attack. Her magical thinking, though, was that she was avoiding an attack by staying within her comfort zone, and staying out of shopping malls and box stores (a huge challenge for agoraphobics because they can't always see the exits). It was more likely that the effect of the panic disorder was lessening, but she wasn't willing to test it out.

It took her longer than the average client to relax enough to even be hypnotized because of her fear of having an attack, but after a couple of sessions of learning to recall pleasant memories and visualize them on a screen while not re-living them, Olivia was ready to get to work.

In a hypnotic trance, but still using the inner screen, she was able to picture her first panic attack at the age of seventeen. It was the night of her senior prom. Her date and their group of friends were hanging out on the huge patio of "one of the rich kid's houses" after the dance. She said, "I wouldn't say we were druggies, but we did like to party, there were no parents around, and somebody had LSD and talked me into trying it."

I asked her to drop into the memory of that experience if only for a moment. I watched her carefully. Her eyes fluttered, and then she gasped and moaned. "That's great, Olivia, now detach and put it all on your screen. You now remember what happened."

She sighed. "At first I thought nothing was happening and then suddenly I was soaring high above my body. I was heading for the stars. I was losing track of where I was … just out further and further away!"

If you have stood outside on a clear night under a southern Arizona sky, you know how bright the stars are and how close they can feel.

She said her heart was pounding at the memory of how freaked out she was, fearing she would never get back into her body. We took a couple of minutes to slow her breathing, and get her heart rate back to normal.

"I don't know how long it lasted, but it seemed to go on and on and on. I thought I was dying."

That night it had taken several hours for her to come down from the experience. Unfortunately, none of the teenagers was brave enough to take her to a hospital where she could have gotten help. She said she would probably have refused to go anyway, because she didn't want her parents to know. But to exist in a state of free fall for several hours made a huge impact.

Dr. Stan Grof's work with patients using LSD as a therapeutic tool to explore the roots of agoraphobia revealed the likely universal fears associated with birth—a feeling of impending catastrophe and annihilation. But this was under controlled conditions and with supportive people, and was therefore helpful. The opposite of what happened to Olivia.

Now throw into that mix the terror of her out-of-the-body (OOBE) experience. Dr. Charles T. Hart made several points about OOBEs in his introduction to Robert Monroe's book, *Journeys Out of the Body:* that they are a universal human experience, that they are generally a once-in-a lifetime event usually induced by great stress, that they are usually one of the most profound experiences of a lifetime, and that most people find them to be a joyful, positive experience. A few are very frightened by them because, while they are happening, they feel as if they are dying. Olivia was thrown into that terrifying experience without any support or context. In her case, the experience triggered panic, which led to more panic attacks, which created the phobia.

It took a few weeks of working on other things before she was willing to return to the experience again. I encouraged her to re-experience the bad trip, but to learn to manage it. That was quite successful. She decided to think of it as an out-of-body experience that she could control. She imagined herself dancing in the stars, spying on her boyfriend, and sitting on top of the roof of the old Spanish-style church in Old Town—each time easily returning to her body. I'm not saying she was having an OOBE; she was using her imagination to work towards diluting her fear. She felt somewhat more confident after that. She was able to imagine herself flying outside her comfort zone, and even to Phoenix, but it wasn't translating into her being able to actually drive her car outside the zone.

At the next session, once in trance (she was comfortable doing that by then), I prompted her to go to the source of the fear of leaving her comfort zone. She reported finding herself in a setting that was definitely not Tucson. She described rolling green hills, a field of colorful wild flowers, songbirds, and some sheep off in the distance. I thought perhaps her inner wise-woman, what I often refer to as the "high-wise self" that can tap into higher wisdom, had pulled up a pastoral image to help her relax or feel peaceful, especially after I asked the usual, "Look down at your feet," and she said there weren't any feet.

"I'm not in a body." Olivia looked confused. I asked, "Is this a metaphor or a memory?" It is remarkable to me that most people can answer that question. She did.

"I'm pretty sure I know this place, but from a long time ago."

A few more questions and she had a clear picture of a young woman called Nonie, living in Ireland in the late 1600s. Her past-life report included scenes of a loving family, a sweet and doting beau, and plans for a summer wedding, close to her seventeenth birthday.

"What happens next?" I asked. She gasped. I asked what was wrong. "The bloody English! Oh, God. No. No!" She got very still.

"Nonie, what has happened?"

She said she didn't know, that everything just went black.

Regression therapists know that if a story is moving right along and then everything just goes black or blank, it usually means that life has come to an end. Processing the death scene is essential to working with past lives, so her not seeing it meant something was amiss.

"Nonie, please progress to moments after your death in that lifetime." She reported what I expected she would. She was back in the beautiful pastoral scene. Now I spoke to Olivia. "How near is this field to Nonie's home?"

"Wow, the little church where she was going to be married is right over the hill."

I asked her to continue speaking from her present-life perspective and see what happened to Nonie, because Nonie had blocked it out. Olivia saw that soldiers had rushed the village, and Nonie had been raped and then her throat cut. Her body had been thrown aside and the marauders moved on. Like many traumatized people, she had dissociated during the rape (often characterized as leaving the body) and then she was killed. My client realized that Nonie was still in that field, staying near the church, and had been there for hundreds of years.

"How is that possible? How can I be here now in Tucson and basically haunting a place near where I was murdered?"

"Let's help Nonie first, and I'll explain later." I assisted her to return to memories of Ireland, and rather than relive her last moments, to just observe them. It was important for Nonie to see her lifeless body so it would sink in that she had died. I don't have any idea why all souls don't automatically make a full transition and return to their spiritual home, but it is obvious that many do not, especially those who die while they are unconscious or dissociated and therefore unaware of what happened. There are also those who stay earthbound for reasons of their own, like those who committed acts for which they fear they will be punished in the afterlife. That is especially terrifying to those who believe in hell or some such after-death place of judgment. I've heard reports of those who stayed around to haunt people out of revenge, and those who stayed around because they couldn't say goodbye to loved ones.

"Nonie, you now see what happened to you. You know your body was destroyed. But you realize your consciousness was not. It is not useful to your soul for a part of it to fail to make the transition." I worked with Nonie for a few minutes until she had fully grasped her situation, expressed grief for what happened to her, and the pain her loved ones felt in losing her. Then she was ready to go. We called on a Being who loved her to assist, and then she was gone.

Now it was time to explain to Olivia how a part of her could be stuck in Ireland while she was alive in Tucson. When I was in graduate school at Arizona State University, we had a visiting professor from Stanford, Dr. Carl Pribram, an authority on the human brain, who told us the mind can handle up to seven bits of information at once. (Now brain specialists are saying from four to nine bits.) One "bit" might be listening to someone talk or working on a math problem. He said to think of our ability to process as like having seven phone lines (this was in the sixties). If they are all busy, there's no chance an eighth bit, like chopping vegetables for dinner or answering your child's question, can be handled until one of the other lines hangs up and is available. Very simplistically, the mind can be in seven places at once. I put that together with a concept introduced in a book by Jane Roberts, the well-known metaphysical writer, poet, and trance channeler of Seth from fifty years ago. Seth said a soul can be in seven realities at once. "In other words," I explained, "If Seth is right, one aspect of your soul is here in Tucson, and perhaps another aspect in a body somewhere else in the world, or in another dimension (as was Nonie), or perhaps even another solar system."

"How about a dog?" Olivia laughed, "I feel like my dog is just like my cousin Hank."

"Yes, that might be possible. I don't think reincarnation is easily explained or even perceived. It's consciousness, and at some level, maybe it is all one consciousness, as some of the great philosophers and teachers tell us.

"Getting back to what might be behind the agoraphobia. When a part of you is lost in space, it is afraid ... afraid of the helplessness of the situation and of not existing outside that reality, like Nonie in her field. I think that night when you took the LSD and had an out-of-body experience, you awakened the memory of Nonie, lost and stuck in an existence she didn't understand, and helplessly could do nothing about. She had an out-of-the-body experience that *did* end in death."

"My god," she said. "I just realized, she was seventeen when she was murdered and I was seventeen when I had that bad trip."

Over the next few weeks, she continued to practice driving (in her mind) outside her comfort zone and hopefully internalizing tools for dealing with panic attacks: remember it isn't dangerous but just her mind responding to a false message, control her breathing, not add to the anxiety with "what-ifs," and do something to distract the brain and wait it out. Even with this practice, she was still fearful of having one.

It came time for the test. A solo drive. The agreement was to drive one mile out of the zone, during low traffic, to a coffee shop with her list of reminders, her water, and her cell phone.

The following week she walked into the office for her appointment with a huge grin on her face. "Guess what? I drove to Phoenix yesterday."

"You did what?" I was stunned. She hadn't planned to go more than the mile. She didn't even wait to sit down to tell me.

"One hour before the big test, I got a call from my aunt that my nephew had been in a motorcycle accident and was in critical care. I had to go. It wasn't easy," she said. "I was scared, and I thought any minute I could have a panic attack, but I didn't. I got there."

She looked a little sheepish when she said she didn't use any of the tools, at least not consciously. (She later realized she had so fully integrated the tools during hypnotic rehearsal that it was automatic.) What gave her courage was talking to her girlfriend on her cell phone and they talked the whole two hours. I asked her if she understood why that helped. She said the moral support was good, but what it really did was keep her grounded in her body. She didn't even start to slip into an altered state or feel any of the warning signs because she was picturing her friend, visualizing what they were talking about, staying focused on the present moment and something other than fear. In effect, she kept her seven lines busy with reaching her goal.

"Anything to get the job done," I said. "Now you know you can do it. Soon you'll do it automatically." She made it to the wedding. She made it back. It wasn't easy for her, but her persistence in rehearsing a positive outcome in her mind over and over, the past-life regression, and hitting on a creative way to break through the fear led to her success.

I'm not the first regression therapist to discover a connection between agoraphobia and a past life in which the spirit was earthbound. It was first described in a doctoral thesis by a colleague, Thelma Freedman, a copy of which she generously gave me. I hasten to add that it has not been my experience that every case of agoraphobia has been resolved through past-life regression, as you will see in the next chapter. Whether the clients didn't stick with me long enough to find all the "lost" parts of their soul, or if there were other causes, I don't have enough information to say. It has shown up in enough cases that I always suggest we explore that possibility.

Chapter 10

The Pathology of Worst-Case Scenario Thinking

So much of what we think and do about risk does not make sense. In a 1990 paper, researchers George Loewenstein and Jane Mather compared people's levels of concern about nine risks—including AIDS, crime, and teen suicide—with objective measures of those risks. The results can only be described as scrambled. 'There is no generally applicable dynamic relationship between perceived and actual risk,' the researchers politely concluded.

> Daniel Gardner,
> *The Science of Fear*

I moved back to Portland in 2005 after having lived in Arizona for eight years. While I feel happy and most connected to the world in the desert, I had missed the culture and the beautiful Willamette River, which divides the east and west sides of the city, with an ache that only getting into the water and paddling around in my kayak could fill. It was the river that called me home. Portland is a soulful city, one that takes good care of its citizens and takes pride in being quirky—bumper stickers urging, "keep Portland weird" abound. Downtown, a whole city block has been turned into what we call our living room—Pioneer Courthouse Square. I've enjoyed a concert with 200 tuba players, served as master of ceremonies for some of the largest anti-war rallies in the country during the first Iraq war, and marveled at the magic when the area is filled with decorated trees, lights, and music during the December holiday season and with roses of every variety during the June Portland Rose festival.

Within ninety minutes one can get to one of the loveliest beaches in the world, or deep into the volcanic mountains of Mt. Hood or Mt. St. Helens. Within a few minutes one can be on an inner city hiking trail or paddling down the Willamette or Columbia rivers. Cultural offerings include plays (I swear we have as many theater companies as churches) or live music (Pink

Martini calls Portland home). Why am I talking about how much there is to enjoy here? Because shortly after my return to The City of Roses, I met a woman who could not enjoy any of those activities. She could not get farther away from her house than four city blocks in any direction. Like my Tucson client, she suffered from agoraphobia.

My office happened to be right at the edge of her safety zone; perhaps that was the reason why she scheduled an appointment with me, but she had a desperate hope that hypnosis could help. A few minutes before her scheduled appointment, she called me, crying and in a panic. She could barely get the words out. "I can't get there. I can't find my keys. I've looked everywhere. For an hour." She apologized and explained it was too far for her to walk, and hoped we could reschedule. Since hers was the last appointment of the day, I offered to come to her house. She breathed a sigh of relief and gave me the address.

Rachel was watching for me out her front window and opened the door as I approached. She looked haggard and her face was flushed. I knew that look; it was the hangover following a panic attack. We had the house to ourselves for at least two hours, plenty of time to get her history and see if hypnosis could work for her.

In her mid-thirties, she was raised in a Jewish household by fearful parents. Her sister, mother, and grandmother also suffered from panic attacks. Some ancestors were in the pograms, the Russian equivalent of the German Holocaust, and she was frequently reminded that the world is not safe. Perhaps in reaction to feeling suffocated by over-protecting and fearful parents, Rachel had lived a highly adventurous life through her teens and twenties "resort hopping as a snow boarder, lots of drugs and bad relationships."

She listed her issues: scared of the dark, scared of having another panic attack and of being too far from home, feeling trapped at home, and recurring disturbing images of people being strung up (hung) in public. She said she hated conflict, adding that her parents have a marriage rife with conflict. She hyperventilates easily and when her throat starts to close up, she goes into panic.

When I asked about previous treatment, she got tears in her eyes. "Two years of exposure therapy. It was a nightmare, and it made me much, much worse. I think it was abusive, what they did to me." I was surprised. I didn't think any legitimate therapist would keep her in treatment that long with only negative results. It turned out it was a free program run by a rotating series of graduate students, each one, it seemed, more eager than the next to be the one to make the breakthrough with Rachel. "Nobody really listened to me when I objected to the things they wanted me to do. They made me feel like a loser, a coward." She had been in law school during all of this. It was astounding that she made it through the program and a tribute to her capacity for hard work.

We had previously discussed by phone that we regression therapists have had some success in treating both panic attacks and agoraphobia with hypnotherapy and past-life regression. She was eager to see what past lives might explain her disorder, and because she was now calm, and appeared to be grounded in her body, we proceeded with hypnosis. I used my usual induction of relaxation of body and mind, and the visualization of descending stairs. She relaxed well, and when I asked her about her stairs. "Coming down, I started to give myself exits." Of course she did. Agoraphobics need to know where the exits are.

I prompted her to go to the major source of her fear. The first story she reported was of being a black child, a boy, living with his parents in North Carolina, in the 1950s. "Dad's a laborer and a lay preacher, a nice man. Mom's nice too, both trying not to make waves. My name is Heathcliff." I thought his mother must have been a romantic who liked literature.

Suddenly Rachel saw Heathcliff's death. Killed by a white mob, but betrayed by his own people. "Father was between a rock and a hard place. He might have saved us if he'd fled town, but he decided to stay and defend himself." He thought members of the church would help, but they were too afraid to stand up to the mob. "We were all hung. He's desperate with guilt. I'm just in shock."

The boy was too young to understand the situation, so we couldn't learn why the family was targeted. We did some healing work with Heathcliff and were successful in getting him out of shock. Rachel created a safe place in her mind's eye for him to rest. She was gratified to learn where the troubling images of people being hanged may have originated.

With a pattern of fear as entrenched as hers, I was sure there was more, so we dug deeper into other lifetimes. The next one she reported was just a snapshot of a white girl, growing up in a rural setting in the upper east coast of America. This time her white father "betrayed the blacks to align with whites. I'm feeling shame and guilt." We revisited the healing place where Heathcliff waited, and worked through the terror, shame, and guilt of those two lifetimes.

What we were exploring, because that's what came up, was the helplessness of being a child (in the past lives, but more importantly in her present) in the midst of racial/cultural tension. I was certainly curious about her soul's journey, given the family into which she was born in this lifetime. Over the next month, her sessions went to darker and darker places. Two of the most disturbing she reported were the story of being a Jewish, gay, black man, locked up in an insane asylum—treated as a sub-human; and of a woman, likely in the early 1800s, who was declared a crazy person, "a raving lunatic, like a junkyard dog," also "thrown into an asylum."

"Wow, this explains my fear of going crazy and being locked up," she said.

She was able to make it to my office for her next appointment. When again prompted to go to the source of the agoraphobia, she reported a past life as a young black woman named Desiree, pretty but with no education or skills, working at a café. Suddenly two white men her boss had earlier refused to serve burst into the café with guns blazing. Rachel looked terrified as she reported: "It's a massacre. I'm the only one left. If he sees me, I'll be shot or worse." Then the picture went blank.

A very visual person, if Rachel said it went blank, it did. That was the end of that life. But obviously Desiree had repressed the tragic ending, the way many people repress memories before, during, and just after a traumatic event. Was this the lifetime that was causing the agoraphobia?

The way to resolve past lives in which death occurred but without the necessary awareness (such as with Nonie in the previous chapter) is to help the past-life person look back, in a detached manner, and view their final moments. Sometimes I need to prompt them to find their body and examine it so they can realize on their own that they had died. Rachel did see the life-less bloody body of Desiree, and understood that she had remained stuck in the scene of her murder. We worked with Desiree, helping her face the truth of what happened and to release the trauma in her body. She also decided to forgive the man who killed her, a decision that frees her from any karmic ties to the perpetrator. Then she was helped to make the transition to her spiritual home base. I gave Rachel the post-hypnotic suggestion that now that Desiree was free, she was also free, and could let the agoraphobia go. Sadly, at her next session, she reported no real change.

Rachel made many connections between triggering present-life circum-stances and past-life trauma, especially the large number of soul experiences of being marginalized and victimized. She felt relief to understand where the deep fears came from. But, unfortunately, in spite of pulling out all the tools I had for helping people manage anxiety and phobias, and all the visualizations and affirmations for her to feel safe, and even though she was no longer hav-ing panic attacks, Rachel was getting worse.

In the process of helping her work through present life issues, I realized that in attempting to feel safe and in control, Rachel would imagine the worst-case scenario. Her rationale was that in imagining the worst, she could imagine herself getting through it. Usually, the worst thing was she'd die. Her mind was frequently flooded with imagined catastrophe, her body in an almost continuous state of fight, flight, freeze mode.

Her youthful risk taking had been counterphobic—she'd been determined not to let fear run her life as it did the lives of her parents. But after her first panic attack, even happy memories, like being an awesome snowboarder, she had re-written in her mind. Very few bad things happened to her during her adventures, but now all she dwelled on were the bad things that *could* have happened. The *what-ifs* had replaced the actual events in her mind. Her thinking, now attuned to worst-case scenarios, was being made worse by piling on the now conscious past-life traumas. We had to stop the hypnosis.

I urged her to get on medication, which she was very loathe to do and I rarely suggest, because she was having a hard time getting to her office. Her doctor gave her a very low dose of Effexor, and that helped a bit. She tried some other alternative therapies, some biofeedback, some spiritual counseling, and was able to get back to the office, but she remained trapped by the agoraphobia.

Fast forward one year, and I'm in a practitioners study group—those of us offering amino acid therapy advice for mood stabilization by supplementing the body's neurotransmitters. I presented Rachel as a case study and we came up with a plan. At first she was afraid to try anything new, especially something that might "mess with my brain." Anyone with a history of panic attacks always worries that a new thing will trigger an attack. But, she agreed to the "pixie dust" approach—opening a capsule of L-tryptophan and placing a tiny bit on the tongue. After a few months of pixie dust, she tried a little GABA. That very evening, she noticed she was able to do something she had not been able to do for seven years—remain in her office, in the evening, alone.

GABA! Nature's stress buster. GABA is an inhibitory neurotransmitter. Julia Ross in *The Mood Cure* describes how GABA operates: "It turns off certain kinds of brain reactions, specifically the production of 'excitatory' chemicals like adrenaline that can become so overwhelming when you are under too much stress." In just one month's time, with a modest dose of this over-the-counter supplement, she was able to go to a large enclosed shopping mall. Unheard of for someone who needed to have an eye on the exits at all times. (See appendix on GABA and other amino acids.)

In her case, knowing where the problems came from, while it made her feel less "crazy," did not resolve them. Feeding her brain something she was deficient in was the first step forward in retraining her mind. It is early in this new treatment, but what I'm expecting is as the agoraphobia is resolved, and she's been free of panic attacks for a couple of years, she'll be able to face those things that she has feared and therefore avoided, and lead a normal life. I'm envisioning her shifting her thinking from *worst case* to *best case*, taking full advantage of the fun, beauty, and weirdness of her adopted hometown.

Chapter 11

Phobias—Spiders, Snakes, Heights, and a Fear of Death

Dr. [Ian] Stevenson's findings give objective credibility to what the past-life therapists have presumed all along—that past-life deaths cause present-life phobias. Many children have phobias that cannot be explained by anything that has happened to them in their present lives. If a parent sees an unexplainable fear in their child, they can now suspect a past-life cause even if the child has made no statement about a past life. That is the way it happened with my children: the phobias appeared before they expressed any conscious memories of their past lives.

Carol Bowman,
Children's Past Lives: How Past Life Memories Affect Your Child

The definition of a phobia is *extreme* and *irrational fear* of an object or situation, often a social situation. See Google for a list of phobias and you'll find Latin names for hundreds of fears, from ablutophobia, the fear of washing or bathing, to zoophobia, fear of animals. Some people are embarrassed by their phobias such as coulrophobia, the fear of clowns. Many would seem to be somewhat reasonable, such as a fear of poison, toxiphobia; or lightning, brontophobia; while others, such as dendrophobia, the fear of trees, are hard to imagine being frightening at all.

Phobias hold people back from pleasurable experiences or exploring new things. They interfere with normal relationships and cause much suffering. How would you ever leave home if you feared trees? How could you live in New York City if you feared enclosed spaces like the subway or elevators? Phobias can be mild or they can be crippling. Sufferers are often met with impatience or disdain by those who have no idea what it is like to have a phobia. Maybe that's how the term irrational came into use?

Probably the notion that the fear is *irrational* occurred because the sufferers cannot identify a reason for the fear. If one day, at the age of four, your drunk uncle Charlie decided to teach you to swim by throwing you into the deep end of the pool, you might be afraid of water or at least of swimming pools. But, unless you generalized that scary experience to *all* water, *everywhere*, or to the point where it was interfering with your life, you wouldn't call it a phobia. It was an understandable learned fear based upon a scary experience, and one that would be easy to overcome with swimming lessons from someone other than Charlie.

Obviously, humans can develop a fear of just about any thing or situation. But why? That's what I wanted to know when I first started working with clients suffering with phobias. What I discovered is that phobias are not irrational at all. Without exception, when a client was willing to explore the cause, we found it. We discovered the original cause, and it was always either from an early childhood (pre-birth included) memory that had been repressed, or from a prior lifetime, and sometimes both.

The very discovery often cured the phobia, or at least greatly reduced its power over the client, in just two or three hours of hypnosis, if the phobia was a simple one, meaning a fear of one specific thing, like spiders or public speaking.

Claustrophobia

A nineteen-year-old university student, Karen, called me to discuss two problems that were getting so bad she was considering dropping out of school and returning home. She'd always had some trouble with enclosed spaces, especially rooms without windows, but it had gotten much worse, to the point she dreaded returning to her dorm room. She also feared the dark. It took her hours to get to sleep and even after dropping off, she would awaken frequently during the night struggling to breathe. She couldn't concentrate and her grades were suffering. She was on a very tight budget and needed to work "efficiently" (her word—I loved it).

In the spirit of efficiency, I spent little time getting her history, learning enough to know hypnosis was appropriate for her. She went easily into a medium trance, and immediately went to the source of both problems. "I'm being buried alive!" She started to hyperventilate. I told her to move out of that body and observe the scene from her present-life perspective. "Okay. I'm seeing a young girl, maybe six or seven years old. I'm not breathing. My father is sobbing. I'm wrapped up tight in a blanket. He digs a hole and lovingly places me in it. Oh, god. He thinks she's dead, but she isn't." (She switched to third person, which is fine. It makes the horror of the situation a little easier to report.)

Karen said that the little girl was jarred into consciousness when she felt the percussion of the shovels full of dirt falling on her body, but by the time she was fully awake her father was gone. She screamed until she ran out of air. With no final thoughts, just abject terror and despair, she died.

I said, "Karen, we can help this little girl, this part of your soul. What would you like to do to help her?" She said, "I want to reach down into that grave and bring her out into the light and fresh air. I want to tell her she's okay." She imagined doing that, and then when the child was ready, she called on the child's guardian angel to move her into the light.

"Now that she's free, you are free. You understand where your fear of closed spaces, your fear of the dark, and your fear of going to sleep all came from. You can now let that all go, as you say goodbye to the child." I closed the session with the post-hypnotic suggestion that she would feel comfortable in any setting, and sleep normally.

She called me the next day and said she had slept beautifully. I followed up one week later, and she reported that the phobia was completely gone. I had no further contact from her, but I did tell her if she needed a reinforcement session in the future to call me. Hopefully no news is good news.

This story makes it evident why exposure therapy may not have helped her, or at least not right away. She believed her phobias were of the dark and of closed spaces, not of taphophobia, the fear of being buried alive. One "efficient" ninety-minute session got to the heart of the issue.

Because she was taking a psychology class and studying the works of Carl Jung, she wondered if it would be reasonable to think of her session as a metaphor, or as imagery for her deep, dark fears, instead of that she had accessed an actual past life. I replied that that is a very reasonable way to look at the experience, and for any type of material that appears as imagery. I don't need to differentiate because my goal for the session is to relieve the symptom. I rely on the wisdom of my client's high-wise self to figure out how. On her way out of the office, she laughed and said she believed it to be a past life, and that worked for her.

Fear of heights

Speaking of efficiency, this client had two phobias she wanted to tackle. I didn't know at the time that she had budgeted for three sessions with me. It is a testimony to the power of intention that her issues were tackled in three sessions. Given their severity and complexity, I thought it might take weeks. Good thing I didn't say that out loud.

Marcella's phobias were a fear of falling from heights, especially while in a car, and a fear of needles, which was making her life miserable because she had a medical condition that required frequent injections.

We started with the fear of heights. She already knew pieces of a past life that she thought might be related. It turned out she was right. It was the story of Lizzie, a woman living in the nineteenth century "wild west" United States. She was forced to work in a dance hall in order to take care of her family (a pattern she recognized in the present). She meets a "good man" and they fall in love. While still courting, he takes her out riding in a buckboard. He is navigating a narrow road high above the river when suddenly the horses get frightened and bolt. "I'm hanging on for dear life, and the horses run off to the right." The buckboard falls off the cliff and she and her sweetheart are killed.

With a fear like hers (heights), there is often more than one past-life story as causal. As I've mentioned previously, the high-wise self knows the answer. I first had her create a healing place inside herself, and then bring Lizzie there. Next I asked my client to visualize a screen in the healing place, like a computer screen, and told her that answers to my questions would appear on that screen. The first question was, "Are there more lifetimes that have contributed to the fear of heights and falling? The answer was yes. "How many?" "Six." "How many of those need to be accessed?" The answer was two. What that told me was the other stories would be similar in nature and belief, and therefore it was unnecessary to retrieve them all.

The next story was of a poor boy in a small village during medieval times. He begged for food as a child and when older got a little work "holding horses for knights and soldiers." (He was either named Page or he was a page; I wasn't sure from my notes.) He finally gets some real training and then at the age of nineteen, "I'm on a battlefield, on a horse. I'm holding a shield in one hand and we're riding fast. We're fleeing. (The client gasps.) I'm falling off the horse and rolling … rolling down a long hill, slamming into rocks! I see my body still. It's over." I gave Marcella a couple of minutes to be with the feelings from that past life and then we moved on.

The final regression was rich and full: the story of Dolly and Thomas. A love story that took place during the historical era of exploration. "We're going to the Colonies (likely the West Indies) to start a new life." George had just completed medical school, and the newly married couple was setting out for an adventure as they began their life together—happy and excited. As they near their destination, the ship falls under attack by pirates. She sobs, "My husband is thrown overboard and I become the property of a violent man." In looking forward a bit, she reports that she is forced to live in his cabin on the ship and only allowed out at night for air. She decides there is no way out of her intolerable situation and finally, in despair, she jumps overboard. "It was freeing and terrifying." The memory of falling, and then drowning, was imprinted upon her soul.

Guided to her healing space, Marcella realized the *energetic memory* of those three past lives, as well as the others not revealed, "led me to constantly brace my body" (when any perceived threat of falling was present). She imagined helping each of those past-life personas, and freeing each of the fearful memory. She then was able to imagine herself crossing over bridges without fear.

A little skeptical as to whether the regression helped, she still made a return appointment to work on the fear of needles. When she arrived for the next appointment she grinned. "It worked. I did drive over a bridge without fear. I told my friend about it, and I said something like the regression might have helped, but time will tell, and my friend jumped all over me. She said not to doubt it. She said I should express gratitude, not doubt. I decided to take her advice." It was good advice. A belief in her ability to heal, and in the healing process, is very helpful in making it so.

Fear of needles (those used for medical injections)

When prompted to return to the source of her fear of needles, a childhood memory appeared in Marcella's mind's eye. "I'm walking home from kindergarten. I'm almost home and a boy is running behind me. He pushed me and I fell onto grass and hit a stake. I see my leg, it's bleeding and my sock is all red. It doesn't hurt. I get up and walk home. My mother sees me and she's very upset. She runs to the neighbors and they take us to the hospital." There is where she was traumatized. She was restrained while her wound was stitched up, her cries of fear and pain ignored. The needle used to numb her leg prior to the stitches seemed huge to the little girl, as was the needle used later to give her antibiotics.

I used a technique called re-framing for this memory. I had her visualize the trip to the hospital, but with the adult Marcella holding the inner child on her lap, quietly explaining everything that was going to happen. The adult participated in helping the child stay calm as the wound was cleaned, imagining that it felt good to have it cleaned. We went through the whole process with each step being easy and then we went through it again this time with herself as the child, being calm and barely feeling the needles. Then I had Marcella imagine taking that same calm feeling into her current situation. She was able to do that, but recognized an underlying resistance out of anger that she had to have injections at all. Again, re-framing was called for. She needed to be out of resentment (which turned into resistance), and into acceptance of "what is." She was able to see the value in acceptance, and shifted her position. At her next session she reported she did well with needles. I reinforced the changes in her beliefs, and left her with the post-hypnotic suggestion that she would continue to be comfortable at any height, and accept injections with ease.

Fear of bugs and snakes

Summer camp can be a great experience for kids, unless they are scared of bugs and snakes. An eleven-year-old had gone to camp the previous summer but an encounter with a small snake, "it zipped past me," ruined it. She had had a good time until then, and was torn between wanting to go back this year and being too scared of the bugs and snakes in residence at the camp. Her mother wondered about hypnosis for her.

Kathleen was an open and friendly girl who was very willing to try hypnosis. In anticipation of her possibly getting frightened during the session, we started by creating a peaceful place in her imagination where she could return as needed. I also included in the induction the prompt to detach from her feelings, and just see what happened, but without emotion. In spite of some pretty horrendous material showing up, she breezed right through the session without a need for her peaceful place. However, what fascinated me was she placed an emergency exit in her stairway (the stairs she visualized at my prompting to deepen her trance). I see this with adults who have high anxiety, usually those who suffer from panic attacks. I felt sad that a child of eleven was already creating ways of coping with high anxiety.

It turned out that the sources of her phobias were all from prior lifetimes. The first one she reported was of being a girl of twelve, Anna, described as wearing a long dress and living in a small western town. She was sitting on the front porch when a large snake started moving across the ground towards her. "I'm scared. I jump up and run to my right—fast—I hit something, a pole. My head is bloody." Then she was silent.

"Anna, now what do you see?" "My parents are crying by the pole. I was killed (by the blow to her head)." Then she described a touching scene at the cemetery where she was buried.

"Good job, Kathleen. Let's take Anna to your peaceful place and ask her to wait. There's more to learn." When she was ready, she easily accessed the next story. This time she was a girl named Elizabeth—between fourteen and fifteen years old and living on the family farm. "My mother ran away from us when I was little. I sweep the stalls, the manure, feed the chickens, and walk the horses. I have a favorite horse, black and brown." In moving her forward Elizabeth said, "My dad just got a phone call. It's about my brother in Australia. A big snake ate him. My heart is beating so hard, it's hurting. I run to my room crying." Her brother was only eighteen years old.

Moving forward again, she reported, "I'm walking around a bale of hay when a black snake scares me. I run into the house and I stay there for the rest of my life. I get stir crazy, then crazy. I can't sleep, I stay up, thinking snakes are all over my house." In despair, Elizabeth kills herself with a kitchen knife.

With loving compassion my young client took Elizabeth to the peaceful place to join Anna. Of course, I was monitoring Kathleen for any signs of trauma—what she reported was horrific—but she had remained emotionally detached from the material and very willing to continue. I felt she was going to benefit from this work, and so we moved on to the next story.

Again, she was a female by the name of Rachel, age twenty and the setting was underwater. "I'm a scuba diver. I'm diving right now. I check the clock on the tank and see I have five minutes of air. Then I realize I'm swimming in a pit full of black eels. I panic and ... I drown."

In looking back over the Rachel lifetime, Kathleen told me Rachel had asthma and used to sky dive with her inhaler "Velcroed" to her glove. I made a note of that. Prior to the unfortunate incident with the eels, Rachel had been a real risk taker, brave and seeking adventure. I could use that memory to help Kathleen access those inner qualities within her self right now.

No wonder this child feared snakes. A lot of prior trauma had piled up, and it only took one small incident, a little garden snake, to throw open the gates of past-life memories. But she also was phobic about bugs. I asked if she was up for looking for that cause and she nodded yes.

The final regression of the session took her to a small cottage, centuries into the past, with a wooden fence, lots of flowers, lots of snakes in the yard, this time as a boy named John, age fourteen. (Snakes didn't bother this boy.) "Mother tells me to take some food to my grandfather." John describes the walk to his grandfather's house, and what he finds when he gets there. "He's lying on the floor and bugs and flies are crawling all over him. He's dead." My young client described the scene in gory detail, including the sound of bugs being squished under John's shoes as he walked towards the body. I was glad Kathleen's mother was not in the room to hear this.

Incidentally, people generally know the gestalt of a past life once it is accessed—they know everything that happened from birth to death, even if they report it in chronological order. In this instance, Kathleen knew that John's grandfather had been shot by a neighbor. John knew who it was, even though that information came to light much later in John's life.

Now Anna, John, and Rachel were in the peaceful space along with present-life Kathleen. We took time with each of them, healing their pain and fear one at a time. I said to Kathleen that she now understood where her fears came from and that she could now let the fears go, using the image of putting the fears in balloons that floated out of sight. I had her imagine the beauty and uniqueness of beetles and snakes, and reminded her that the bugs and little snakes where she lives and at the beach are harmless. I told her to remember Rachel and John's courage and to bring that courage into her present mind and body. Then I crossed my fingers. The power of belief is everything. I hoped that Kathleen believed.

A week after the session I got this e-mail from her mother:

The first couple of days were rough. She was worried that what she experienced wasn't real and that she was making it up. I encouraged her to not focus on that piece of her experience. I reminded her that you did not have her relive her experiences and that you kept her at a safe distance so that it may have felt more surreal than real. This seemed to help her. We got her the 5-HTP [an amino acid used for mood regulation and better sleep] *and that has helped greatly! She has been falling asleep before eleven, which is her usual time, and she is sleeping more soundly. Also, she brushed a bug off of me at a picnic almost absentmindedly, whereas usually she would have screamed hysterically if there was a bug on me. This was incredible. My stepbrother received a toy snake as a gift and Kathleen just smiled. He put it on his shoulders and this typically would have sent her into a panic, and it did not. She seems to be doing better. I really appreciate the work that you did with her.*

I recommended a one-hour follow-up to reinforce her courage, and following that appointment, Kathleen requested her mother take her to a pet store so she could touch a snake. That was amazing. The last I heard, she was signed up for camp.

Chapter 12

Eating Disorders

Nearly 10 million females and 1 million males in the US are battling eating disorders such as anorexia and bulimia, while millions more suffer from binge eating disorder. The peak onset of eating disorders occurs during puberty and the late teen/early adult years, but symptoms can occur as young as kindergarten. More than one in three normal dieters progresses to pathological dieting.

www.nationaleatingdisorders.org

Whether it is overeating, bingeing, fearing fat, carbohydrates, or protein, being desperate to feel full, or desperate to avoid eating, there are millions of people in the United States with a pathological relationship with food. With the highest death rate among people with mental illnesses, eating disorders are poorly understood by mainstream medicine aside from the belief they are a combination of biology and environment. The emotional component—the underlying beliefs—has been of great interest to me, and over the years, I've seen how pre-birth and past-life experiences have contributed to the disorder. All of the case histories I report here are of female clients because mainly women have sought my help for these issues. Men also have eating disorders but unfortunately many men feel this is a "female problem" and are too ashamed to ask for help. Sad to say, there are also many fewer resources for men. (See appendix for useful resources for men and women.)

Overeating

With obesity, the stories are similar. Sufferers have tried diet after diet without success and their issues with food often started at a young age. When prompted to go to the source of their need to overeat, one of three scenarios is reported: starvation, deprivation/abandonment, or sexual abuse.

Ellie, a grandmother, knew more about nutrition than most people and seemed to eat healthy food; she just ate too much, too often. She was painfully critical of herself for "being weak and pathetic." Medical issues were piling up: high blood pressure, diabetes, aching joints, and her husband worried she had sleep apnea.

In hypnosis, when prompted to go to the primary source of the issue, Ellie reported a past life as a female in an Amerindian tribe in the northeastern part of the United States.

It was late fall and they had been accumulating food for the winter when an early storm caught them by surprise. Those who had remained in the camp retreated to their winter cave quarters, also where the food was stored, and waited for the men to return from their big fall hunting trip. The storm lasted for days, trapping the women, children, and the elderly men inside the cave.

My client said they strained their ears, hoping to hear the sound of their men returning with food, but after several weeks, she figured either they had had to seek shelter to survive and they wouldn't return until a thaw, or they hadn't survived. Eventually they used up their inadequate stores, and the old ones and children began dying.

"I'm holding my daughter close to my heart." Sobbing desperately she cried, "She's only three, and so weak now she's stopped crying. I can't bear it!" Suddenly she realizes the child in her lap is her granddaughter in her current life.

"Now I understand why I throw food at her if she's the least bit tired or irritable. My daughter gets all over me for that." The Indian woman's dying thoughts were of the searing pain at seeing loved ones die of starvation, and of her own desperate hunger. She vowed she would *never go hungry,* nor would anyone she loved.

Like I said earlier, if you're a boomer or older, you know where you were the day John Kennedy was shot. Everyone knows where they were on 9/11. We are hardwired to remember emotionally charged events, from this life and from past lives. In just that way, emotionally charged vows made at the time of death strongly imprint upon the soul. I surmise that behind most obsessions we'd find past-life vows, pledges, and highly charged emotional trauma. Just imagine what havoc is played with one's love life, if in a past life your final words to your lover were "I will never love anyone but you." For eternity? Excluding all others?

Once Ellie understood why, in her present life, she forced food on her family and ate as if there would be nothing in the cupboards tomorrow, she was able to accept a reasonable food plan. Working with a nutritionist and me, and using smaller dinner plates, she began to lose weight.

Another client, who also tried to eat healthy food, mostly vegetarian, said she felt a little crazy because she never felt full. "I finish a meal, and then I take seconds, even for breakfast." It wasn't that she was still hungry, it was that she had this "voice" inside her that wanted more.

In her regression, Francesca reported a lifetime as a small boy living in a middle eastern country (my client thought it might be modern Pakistan). He'd not known his father, and his mother died of an illness when he was about five or six years old. No one came to help him and he wandered the streets, eating whatever scraps of food he could find or steal. Too young to survive on his own, he reported falling down in a gutter in a monsoon rainstorm, so hungry he was hallucinating—a feast, tables laden with food as far as he could see. His dying thought was "I'll never go hungry again." Francesca wept with compassion for that poor and neglected child and had the thought that she had been eating for him all these years. "It was his hunger that was *insatiable*."

We worked with (the image) of the little boy, with an outpouring of love, and then she released him to what she called his guardians. The change in Francesca was astonishing. She reported that the feeling of insatiability was gone. She was able to eat a moderate amount of food and feel full.

"Just to prove to myself that the little starving boy inside me is really gone, I always leave a little food on my plate at the end of my meal." That kind of small ritual around the life-changing experience makes it even stronger and deeper.

The second common scenario at the core of eating disorders is of deprivation, and reported in lifetimes of too little food for too many mouths, or too little love (food is often a substitute for love). This young woman was plagued with a binge disorder. Amelia was not seriously overweight, but her self-esteem was low. She felt unattractive and longed for a relationship, which she didn't believe was possible at her current weight. The pattern was that as soon as she got into her car after work, her mind started obsessing about treats. When the obsession overtook her, there was no part of her that could say no to eating several maple bars and a package or two of Oreos in one sitting.

In a hypnotic trance, Amelia was prompted to go to the source of this need to binge. The story of a thirteen-year-old Polish girl named Helen appeared in her mind's eye. The year was 1942 and she was captured and taken to a concentration camp. She reported doing hard manual labor in the camp, like moving rocks in a wheelbarrow.

"I'm so angry. Others (prisoners) are nice to me, a girl talks to me nicely, but there's never enough to eat. I fight for food. I push people aside to get food when it's on the ground."

When prompted to move forward she said the camp was closing. "We are liberated, but I don't know where to go." A soldier offered her a ride in the sidecar of his motorcycle. He took her to a military post (she thinks it was American), and then to a church with what appeared to be other survivors, but she was uncomfortable with all the fussing over her.

"Too much attention. I run away. I couldn't handle it." She found work churning butter and doing laundry for a woman in exchange for a sleeping palette and bread and potatoes but she didn't stay there long.

Returning to the city, which she said was in rubble, she bumped into that same officer who had given her a ride when she was released from the camp. This time he took her to his little house where "he lets me take a bath and wash my clothes and sleep in a real bed, and," she sighed, "he leaves me alone." After she rested she went downstairs and burst into tears at what she found. "The table is full of food just for me. *I want to eat it all*. I want to but I can't because he's watching." I asked her to look at her body and describe it. "Bones and skin." She thought about the food and worried whether there would be more tomorrow. "I want to take rolls to my room just in case, and later I sneak back and take some food." She felt better eating alone.

Fifteen or sixteen years old and alone in the world, Helen struggled daily to survive. The memory of profound joy and relief at being offered a table full of food was imprinted upon her soul. That, along with Helen's anxiety, explained why my client in her present life binged to relieve all of her uncomfortable thoughts and feelings.

Amelia e-mailed the day following the regression to Helen's story. "I started overeating after being in Europe. I was traveling on a train through Germany and Austria when I was startled awake by a conductor speaking German. In panic, my first thought was *I'm not Jewish*." Raised Protestant, she said she had always felt an inexplicable need to carry on Jewish traditions.

Over the next few weeks, Amelia accessed six additional past lives of various forms of deprivation, explaining why the binge pattern was so strong. She worked to heal them all. But Helen's story was at the core. One of the challenges she faced in her present life in recovering from the eating disorder was that her brain was used to being flooded with carbohydrates on a regular basis. So in addition to hypnosis, I recommended she consider certain supplements (amino acids) plus plenty of protein to improve her mood and tame her cravings. She worked hard and soon found she had the will power to stop eating sugary, starchy junk food, and to end the emotional torment that came with bingeing.

Overeating to gain power and safety

There's a strongly held belief in the recovery field that some people, as a result of having been sexually molested as children, gain excess weight as adults. There are many anecdotal stories to back up that theory. Why is that? When I've regressed sexual abuse survivors with weight issues back to the event of the molestation, they share one or both beliefs: "It happened because I was pretty or cute" (most likely because the abuser told them that), or "it happened because I was too small to stop it." In both cases, the children found a reason which made sense to them (no matter that it wasn't true), and which made them feel less powerless. The thinking is, "If it is because I'm pretty or cute, then I can become less attractive and I'll be safe. If it happened because I'm small, then I'll get as big as possible and then I'll be safe."

But what about people who hold those beliefs but weren't sexually abused? Of course, many people repress traumatic childhood memories. So, when taking the history of a new client with serious weight issues, if there are symptoms suggestive of childhood abuse, I do ask a lot of questions. I'm very careful in the way I question, especially when the client is in a hypnotic trance, so as to not create "false" memories. False memories are those created in the imagination of a client when asked direct questions such as "was it your uncle?" or "did you feel scared?" The client pictures what was asked, and it automatically becomes part of the story. But, if the client wasn't raised in a chaotic environment, or one with other abuses such as physical or emotional abuse and neglect, and if there aren't any stories of sexual addiction or abuse in their extended family, and the client feels confident there was no abuse, we'll look elsewhere for answers for the *emotional component* of their obesity.

Such was the case with Hannah, who was easily one hundred pounds overweight, but whose biological parents and siblings were of average weight. It seemed as if she had had a fairly trauma-free childhood aside from teasing for being overweight. When I prompted her to go to the source of her weight issues, three past life stories were reported.

The first took place homesteading in the early 1800s in the American Southwest. She reported she was a four- or five-year-old girl. The family compound was attacked by Indians. While her parents and brothers fought back, she and a sister just a little older than her, hid in the house. Suddenly two men came in through the window and snatched the two little girls and carried them off. Her thought in that terrifying moment was "I'm too little." Too little to fight, too little to protect herself. She and her sister were taken to a village and made slaves. She died young, Hannah said, of hopelessness. The memory of that past life was awakened in her present life when Hannah was about five years old and some older boys made her play cowboys and Indians. The other two past lives were in a similar vein, each short lived and ending with the erroneous belief that her negative fate was because of being small and helpless.

Her treatment moved quickly once she found the source of her underlying belief that being big equaled being safe. Progression therapy worked well for her; that is, she could imagine a future, one year ahead, in which she was more slender and yet felt strong and safe. Being able to imagine that gave her the inspiration to stick with her meal and exercise plan. She also reported that pounds did start to drop off with little effort when she focused on feeling powerful. In addition to losing weight, her focus on feeling powerful extended into other parts of her life. She was promoted at work, with a substantial raise and she was firmer with her children. "I never thought I could get my eleven–year-old to stop sassing me. When I changed, she changed. How cool is that?"

Restricted Eating

Anorexia is the most bewildering of the eating disorders when trying to find a *reason* for a person to restrict their food intake. I've personally only worked with a handful of women with this disease in my private practice, and less than fifty when I was part of the treatment team at a holistic residential eating disorders program. I don't yet have a coherent theory that explains the emotional aspect of the disorder, although I suspect it is very diverse. The most fascinating case I encountered was a young mother of three girls who was so underweight that she barely made the requirement to be in the program. Any less and she would have been hospitalized instead. She was very motivated to get well because she did understand that she was starving her body and her brain. She was there because of her children.

This woman was quite religious (Jewish) and she was uncomfortable with the idea of hypnosis, let alone a past-life regression, but her primary therapist had referred her to me. I explained that many residents found hypnotherapy helpful, and some specifically requested regression therapy, but it was up to her. I also explained that one could think of this process as relaxation of the body and conscious mind, while allowing the unconscious mind to come up with stories and images to help with her treatment. She agreed to give it a try.

In her first session, she relaxed very well, and we spent a little time looking at food and body image issues that developed when she was a child. She was clearly able to remember and to visualize, so I suggested she go a little deeper, and find the source of her desire to restrict. She gasped and sat up in the chair (a very rare occurrence) and said she wanted to stop. I asked what happened and she said she suddenly felt like she was in a concentration camp. Disturbed by the image, she decided that it had to have been something her father or grandparents had spoken of. I said that was certainly possible, but I encouraged her to consider what that image might represent. I didn't press her to continue but to let me know if she wanted to go further. Two days later, after talking with the clinical director and her roommate, she said she wanted to try again.

Back in trance, I encouraged her to return to the story she had previously glimpsed, but start the story at an earlier, happier time. She reported living in a large and comfortable apartment, with a successful and hardworking husband and their baby girl. As she got more details, we learned they lived in Germany, that they were Jews, and her name was Anna. She wept as she spoke of their arrest by Nazi soldiers and then of being separated from her husband as they were loaded into trucks.

The next scene was being in a barrack with other women with children. Her little girl was small, maybe one or two years of age when they first arrived at the camp. She was there for at least a year, maybe more, when one day she reported finding a little food.

"I'm so happy I can give my daughter a little more food today. She's growing and needs it." Anna explained that she got two rations a day, one for her and one for the child. "I give my daughter most of the food. *I eat as little as possible to just survive*, for her sake." We both gasped out loud at that comment. I asked my client, "Did you hear what you just said?" She burst into tears. "Oh my god, I get it; my daughter then is my middle daughter now, and I would do anything to keep her alive. She's got some problems."

Some kind of reverse magical thinking was going on at a subconscious level in her present life. *"I love my daughter and it is up to me to see that she survives. In order to do that, I will eat only enough to subsist."*

Sadly, neither Anna nor her daughter survived the Holocaust. I prompted her to move past her death and to take a look at how that past life might be the etiology of the eating disorder. She felt certain it was. That session marked a major turning point in her recovery.

Spiritual DNA

Traumatic events, indeed any highly emotionally charged experience in past lives, leave imprints within what might be called one's spiritual DNA. It appears to me that some food allergies and sensitivities were created in past lives. Take the client who, when prompted to discover the source of her allergy to dairy products, reported a past life when she died a painful death after drinking milk—highly possible prior to pasteurization. A woman with an inability to drink water (her throat would start to close up even thinking about taking a drink of water) traced that phobia to a past-life drowning.

I wish I could make the claim that regression therapy heals eating disorders, but it doesn't on its own. As you have seen, regressions can reveal possible reasons for the disorder, and this therapy, along with general hypnotherapy, is a positive companion to cognitive and nutritional treatment. In the case of anorexia, I highly recommend residential treatment and closely supervised aftercare, along with group and individual therapy.

Chapter 13

The Limiting Beliefs from Past-Life Trauma Carried into the Present

> The subconscious mind is strictly a stimulus-response playback device; there is no "ghost" in that part of the "machine" to ponder the long-term consequences of the programs we engage. The subconscious works only in the "now." Consequently, programmed misperceptions in our subconscious mind are not "monitored" and will habitually engage us in inappropriate and limiting behaviors.
>
> Bruce H. Lipton,
> *The Biology of Belief*

Core beliefs live in the subconscious mind. Bruce H. Lipton, in his book, *The Biology of Belief*, says that as children we pick up perceptions from others, like parents or teachers, which we assume are true. "Their perceptions become hardwired into our own brains, becoming our 'truths.'" He continues: "Here's where the problem arises: what if our teachers' perceptions are inaccurate? In such cases, our brains are then downloaded with misperceptions." In other words, there's nothing in the subconscious that determines whether beliefs are true or false. Therefore programmed misperceptions, as he says, will habitually engage us in inappropriate and limiting behaviors.

Our work as adults is to challenge all beliefs behind inappropriate and limiting behaviors, and use the free will that is ours to change them. That's hard enough to do. Now add into that mix all the beliefs carried over from prior lifetimes, which feel true but are most certainly not true for the current lifetime.

According to the psychiatrist and eminent past-life regression specialist Dr. Brian Weiss, "The scope of the past must be enlarged to include past lives if uncovering the present lifetime's sources proves unsuccessful." I agree with him when he says that only when *all* sources of the problem are brought to light can the person be healed.

The Fear of Making Decisions

It doesn't take long for a client to reveal his or her core issues. It is one of the reasons I love hypnotherapy. I learn how clients approach life—what motivates them and what holds them back—by how a client interacts with me and their *inner world*, and I see much of it within the first few minutes of a hypnosis session.

Nancy scheduled a past-life regression hoping to understand how she undermined her own success. During the first few minutes of the regression, she frequently asked me, "is it okay?" prior to answering a question.

"Is it okay that the stairs curved to the left?"

"Is it okay that I feel like laughing?"

Several times, when I asked a question, she'd respond and then apologize for the answer. My standard way of moving a client into a past-life story is having them imagine proceeding through a passageway. I suggest they move to the exit, and then I count them through, "3, moving to the exit, 2, stepping through, 1, feet planted in another time." This works for most people, most of the time. Then I ask what they know so far, focusing primarily on the place. "Indoors, outdoors, or …" What she said was "I didn't keep up with you because there were two passageways, one that was open and one that had a door that was locked, and I was trying to decide what to do. I'm sorry."

I explained that there was nothing to be sorry about and that I found the imagery interesting and something to be explored.

"Well, what I decided to do was take the door that wasn't locked."

"And what did you notice?" I asked.

"When I stepped through the open door, I was welcomed by a loving Being … and then everything went blank."

"What were you thinking as you stepped through that exit?"

"That maybe I should have chosen the other door."

Second guessing herself, distrust of her own response and the imagery that showed up, and worst of all judging her response as likely wrong—all are highly suggestive she was intellectually abused as a child or was now in an abusive relationship or both. No matter what Nancy thought she came to see me about, the only thing to explore in this session was how she came to have so little faith in her own thoughts, beliefs, and feelings. This likely explained her lack of personal success—she was paralyzed when it came to trusting herself about anything, especially to make a decision.

We needed to delay the past-life regression in order to deal with this lack of self-trust. I asked more questions about her childhood and learned that both parents abused her, verbally, emotionally, and physically. She said she'd had a lot of therapy already because of that abuse. But what she hadn't considered, because it isn't addressed much, is the profoundly destructive *intellectual abuse* that causes a child to distrust her own thoughts and perceptions.

I prompted her to go to the source of her lack of self-confidence, and she went back to age five.

"It's scary in the house, I don't get the rules, I can't do anything right, I can't do anything well enough, Mother doesn't think I'm pretty, and Father thinks I'm bad" (especially when he used a belt on her, I learned later). I suggested that adult Nancy scoop up that child and tell her none of what they told her was true, and we were here to help her change those awful beliefs about herself. Fortunately, Nancy felt compassionate towards her small self, and understood how a five-year-old could believe negative messages. We went through each belief and changed it to a positive one. She vowed she would work on trusting her inner self more.

At her next appointment, Nancy felt prepared to "go with what shows up" rather than questioning it. Once she obtained a medium trance state, she reported: "I'm surfing down through the sky. It's like I'm in a cartoon, a little boy skimming over the tops of European buildings and landing in a cobblestone street. I'm barefoot, wearing rags, *Clamation*™ hands. It's the Dark Ages. I have an alcoholic father who yells, there's a woman, not my mother, who is afraid of my father. Everyone fears the evil town sheriff, but ... I'm surrounded by good people. I'm not afraid and it is a good life."

I praised her for allowing such a story to show up for her, and for not questioning or blocking it. I consider cartoon-like imagery, or fantasy-like stories such as hers, to be the mind playing it safe. It is, again, the brilliance of the higher self to know what will work. She needed to start building trust by having an experience that couldn't be refuted. It isn't real so she can't possibly make a mistake. Plus, fairy tales are archetypal, and always helpful. Nancy could identify with the little boy who, in spite of bad parents and an evil sheriff, felt safe, loved, and happy. It was a good start.

After a few sessions of work on her present-life trauma, she still hadn't changed her beliefs about herself to any significant degree. Like Dr. Weiss said, we needed to look deeper and find all the sources by looking at past lives.

No cartoons this time, and she didn't block the material by questioning it either, "I'm a young man, age twenty-two, walking along a cobblestone street. I have a knapsack and I'm traveling. I want to see what's out there."

He had left home at age eleven and had been on the move since then. "The secret is to be in the *now*—good ale, good wenches." He did odd jobs to earn his food, lodging, and ale: chopping wood, sharpening knives, and moving cargo at the dock. "I get hit over the head, out cold, and next thing I know I'm on board a ship, shanghaied. Now I'm not free. I hoped to get the captain to trust me and then escape, but instead I'm beaten to death and then tossed overboard."

When Nancy looked at the face of the captain, she recognized the soul, "It's my present-life mother. She really hates me. She wants to destroy me."

It's important to follow the thread. What's the source of the animosity between her and her mother? In answer to that question, the story of Thomas showed up. A medieval setting, he was a happy young man, well loved by family, and with friends who enjoyed running around, competing at archery, and doing other masculine endeavors. He fell in love with a pretty girl. One day he was bringing her a rabbit for supper when a small group of soldiers approached on horseback. Playfully, one of them grabbed the girl and Thomas rushed to help.

"They brush me off, and I'm enraged. I grab my sword, but before I can strike a blow, he runs me through. I see the same face as the captain. It's my mother again."

Intrigued, I suggested Nancy move in between lives and connect with her higher self and guides in order to get a deeper understanding of her mother's hatred.

She reported that her guides said, "We wanted to show you lives of freedom, joy, suffering, and pain, as well as gratefulness. As for your mother? It started here." She was guided into a past life.

Nancy said, "She (meaning her present-life mother) is a female, in a bridal gown, and I'm the groom. I believe her to be weak and helpless and that I am doing her a big favor by making her my bride. But instead of being grateful, she rejects me. I'm enraged by the rejection and I kill her. I just lost it.

"I get it now. How this all fits. I started it, with arrogance, thinking I knew what was best, and then losing it when she rejected me. It's an awful, indescribable feeling to lose your mind and take a life. Then we meet up again in another incarnation, this time she/he started messing with my girl and again I became enraged. This time I'm the one who got killed, and then again in the next life, the captain killed me. I guess mother's soul just never forgave me, and lifetime after lifetime has sought me out to hurt me. Now I'm afraid to seek my freedom, to be on my own, to make decisions, because she got to me so young. In fact, I must have realized who she was even before I was born. I felt doomed, hopeless, and I didn't trust myself. Oh, yeah. Play it safe. Make no mistakes by making no decisions. Just survive. I've done that my whole life."

A few more weeks of work, and she felt she had made amends to her mother at a soul level and cut the karmic tie by declaring she was done with the victim/perpetrator pattern. She began to set boundaries with her parents and forgave herself for her past mistakes and timidity. She gained self-confidence and started seeking out opportunities for ways to support herself. She wasn't ready to take a hard look at her marriage yet, but I have hope that she will find the courage to do that eventually.

Taking the blame for the death of others

I've seen numerous examples of people who were afraid to make decisions, and when prompted to the source reported one or more lifetimes when they made a decision that resulted in a painful death (theirs or others) or humiliation. One client whose wife complained because he deferred all decisions to her, reported during his regression:

"I'm leading a wagon train through the Rocky Mountains, against the advice of others because of the late start, when an early snowstorm traps us. Every member of the group died." His dying thought was he shouldn't trust his own judgment ever again. Remember how powerful those dying thoughts are, especially when they begin with "never again."

It is often the case that a person takes responsibility for a tragedy that was an accident or out of their control. A woman overprotected her children and never let them out of her sight except while they were in school. Her frustrated husband finally insisted she get help. When prompted to go to the source of her fears about her children, a tragic past life appeared. She was the mother of a child who was kidnapped from a park near their home and murdered. She blamed herself for the decision to let the child go out to play.

Emotional flooding

Floreid seemed to collapse under even the slightest hint of confusion, such that if more than one of her four children wanted her attention at the same time, she'd scream at them to leave her alone and rush to the bathroom and lock the door. Her sister got her attention by saying she should call in the

Nanny (referring to the reality TV show) to see how crazy she acted. This sister expressed concern that Floreid's behavior was abusive. (I applaud her for that. Abused children need an advocate.) That got her in to see me. It is devastating to wake up to the fact you are scaring your children. She discovered the source of what we identified as "getting emotionally flooded and overwhelmed."

She reported a past life as a little girl living in a village in medieval Scotland that was overrun by fierce invaders, "like a scene out of the movie *Brave Heart*," she said. Her little body was flooded with terror from the noise of shouting and screaming, the pounding sound of the horses, the smoke and fires, the utter chaos and confusion. She screamed and screamed in terror as she ran, looking for her mother. This client was born with a *panic response to confusion.*

Several more lifetimes had to be explored, as this was a very ingrained pattern. In addition, she needed behavioral therapy to learn to manage her emotions. I referred her to a clinic specializing in Dialectical Behavior Therapy (DBT) for that help. It was a stormy process for her, but after two years of hard work, she now is in better control of herself, and best of all, she is enjoying being a mother.

Afraid to See

An immigrant from South America, Maria came to one of my workshops on self-hypnosis. She wanted to learn to reduce her anxiety and hoped to gain some tools. I broke the group into dyads to practice the induction technique on each other and to learn how it feels to be in a light trance. Within minutes of the practice session, her partner called me over to their side of the room. She whispered to me, "I think this lady is in trouble, and I don't know how to help her." Maria was trembling and short of breath. I knelt down beside her and told her to open her eyes and focus on me. Once I felt she was grounded, I asked her what was going on. She said she didn't know, but as soon as her partner told her to envision going down stairs she started to feel scared and then everything went black. I asked if that had ever happened to her before and she said no. Since it was a short workshop on self-hypnosis, not a therapy group, I couldn't help her in the moment. I recommended she and her partner trade places, and that she schedule a private session with me as soon as possible.

I figured the experience had triggered a traumatic memory, and I wondered if it had something to do with her reason for fleeing her country. I hoped she would call, as I didn't like the idea that she would be left with that disquieting experience. I was pleased when she did.

I spent quite a bit of time easing her into a relaxed state, reassuring her that I would be with her every step of the way. Again, just as in the workshop, when she visualized starting down stairs, the inner picture went black.

Now, black is not *nothing*. If I know a client can visualize and suddenly things go black, something is happening. I asked her to use other senses "feel around, listen, use your intuition."

She frowned. "I might be buried in a building."

"And it is too dark for you to see?"

"No, I'm afraid to see."

I wanted to get a better perspective of the situation and being in the middle of a traumatic event is a bad time to be asking questions, so I asked her to go back a few hours. That worked. She was now able to visualize herself as a little girl between six to ten years old.

"I'm wearing a nice striped dress and a hat. I'm next to my dad on the porch of our house. I feel afraid of something." (Now she was ready to see what happened to her.) "An earthquake." (She gasped.) "I can't move. I can't talk. I am buried in the building and … I have polio."

In that brief experience, Maria realized where her fear came from. The little girl was not just buried in the rubble of her basement; she was unable to move to help herself because of the polio. She apparently died there. Maria had seen enough, and reported that the girl "went into the light, the sweet, sweet light. She went to heaven."

I trust the process of regression. I'm not in charge of what shows up, I just ask questions. Often, in one session, both the source of a problem and a path to healing will appear. That's what happened to Maria. The next past-life story she reported was of being born into a noble family.

"I'm a prince and live in a castle." He was brimming over with pride and happiness as he described his beautiful mother, and the fun of watching people dancing at the ball. As he grew older, he was trained to use a bow and fight with a sword. He felt strong and competent. He died young on the battlefield, but with pride. "I was a brave man."

Anna felt excited to access the feeling of being strong, competent, and brave. "As a woman, I have sometimes felt like the little crippled girl, afraid, cautious, maybe even helpless."

I observed, "It's important for women to develop their masculine traits. Take that princely part of yourself home with you today. It's time for you to see. To see yourself in a new way."

Nobody loves me

"Last night I had a feeling of despair, a well of thought that nobody loves me." Phillipa, an actress, said she believed it was irrational because it seemed like a lot of people did love her, but "I look for evidence that they really don't." She said it was possible she was born with that feeling and wanted to explore it through a regression.

The lifetime reported was set in the early part of the 20th century in Florida. "I'm working at a resort as a waiter. My name is Roger and I'm thirty-one, unpleasant, sleazy, greasy dark hair, trying to pass myself off as one of the [upper class] crowd. I want to move up, to travel. I had a girl once, but she split."

I learned he'd fled New Jersey to avoid taking care of his ill mother. He started to talk about hanging out with guys and present-life Phillipa said, "He might be gay," and then *he* said, "I don't want to talk about it." His story continued with lots of drinking and moves from job to job. He was pretty guarded as he talked about some altercation with a broken bottle. All he said was, "I can't afford to get arrested again." Just wanting a room and three meals, he enlisted in the navy. "I'm on a warship. Not what I had in mind. I look at someone but I have to be careful (another reference to being gay). I've got nobody here, but I've got the guys." He liked the honor that existed in the service, and one of his most pleasant memories was attending a ceremony where some fellow sailors were given awards.

As his navy career came to an end, he reported, "I have a companion." They lived in France for three months but returned to New York because his companion fell ill. I asked if they were lovers, and he said, "We don't do that." But he was touched when his friend gave him a ring. "Nobody ever gave me anything like this before." In moving forward he reported he was in the hospital where his companion died. "I walk away from nothing."

The last scene was Roger's own death. "I'm in a shelter, out on the streets again. I have no address. I tell my stories over and over to the guys here." Looking back over that lifetime, my client had regrets. "I wasn't there for Mom like my dad was; I drank too much; I didn't show up. I was a coward, disgusted with myself." And, I thought to myself, *he denied his homosexuality, even to himself.*

Coming out of trance, my client reported she was surprised to learn that her core issue was not so much about distrusting people who say they love her, as not recognizing love when it was there. We worked on opening her heart to let love in. I ended the session with the post-hypnotic suggestion that she would notice and accept with gratitude all evidence of those who love her for being herself.

Fear of Being a Healer—Heretics and Witches

There are common archetypal themes that show up in my practice. Because of my previous two books about clients' reports of past lives during the time of Christ, I have worked with numerous people who resonate with what I've come to call the *archetypes of the Holy Family*. The second most frequent archetype to show up is that of the *persecuted healer.*

The typical phone call to me starts with "I feel called to be a healer in this lifetime but something always stops me." Be it becoming a doctor, nurse, therapist, or using their natural gifts of hands-on healing or clairvoyance, each person feels blocked—by circumstances like the inability to get financial help for school or lost paperwork from the admissions office; giving in to a family which disdains their choice—or by self-sabotage. These kinds of cases come in waves. It is something I can't explain, but in 2006 I saw over two-dozen people with this specific issue. I collected those cases together and started writing a book I would call *Heretics and Witches,* but when I transcribed the case notes, I discovered there were not twenty-five stories, just basically one or two stories with slight variations. So I decided rather than a book, it would be included in this chapter.

The protagonist in the story is almost always a young woman. The locales are in Europe during the Middle Ages. Most of the time she was taught the art of healing by her grandmother or a motherly figure. Some gave more details than others, but often there were scenes of identifying and collecting plants for healing and instructions on making healing oils, teas, and salves. There was always a feeling of love and admiration held for her mentor. Most of the reports included a deep spiritual connection to the natural world. Sometimes they said the plants would speak to them. I'd ask them to recall an especially gratifying healing experience, and I'd hear touching stories of these women helping members of their community through their ministrations. Sometimes they practiced in the open without fear in the beginning, but then there was a change in the community, a new religion or new political position on healing, with disastrous results. Sometimes they practiced in secret and in fear of being caught.

Claire wanted to study to be a midwife, but she had failed the entrance exam twice, the first time because she procrastinated studying and just wasn't prepared, and the second time she showed up a day late for the exam. A friend gently suggested she might be sabotaging herself, and she took that to heart and called me.

Her past life was told through the eyes of a woman who had delivered most of the babies in her part of town, and all the women still asked for her. But the town physician (a man) had been successful in making the practice of midwifery illegal. Even so, she simply could not turn away from the knock on her door in the middle of the night. Of course she got caught, was arrested, and thrown into prison for the rest of her life. She died in that cold, dark cell with the thought that *being a healer* cost her her life. In Claire's present life, the subconscious belief was: it is dangerous to be a healer. That explained her self-sabotage.

In accessing that past life, she was able to change the belief—to update the information that there's an honored place for midwives today, and that it isn't just safe to be a healer today, but it's an honor and a privilege. After the regression, she prepared for the test and went on the correct day. She was admitted to school, and I trust she has become happy and successful in her career.

Burned at the Stake

The most horrific of the stories, though, were those that happened during the period called the Inquisition, when people, mostly women, were declared either heretics or witches and imprisoned, banished, hanged, or burned at the stake. Those stories were almost unbearable. I heard past-life stories from the point of view of the victims, and of those who witnessed the killing of a mother or grandmother, or a beloved male or female healer. Sometimes the victim was simply old, demented, or mentally ill but declared possessed by the devil.

There is a lot of misinformation about those times; for instance, there's a strongly held belief that as many people were killed as witches or heretics as were killed during the Holocaust. There's no evidence that the numbers are even close to that. According to research done by Dr. Richard J. Green as reported in his article, "How Many Witches?", an estimate made by studying actual records is about 100,000 people over two centuries. However, one is too many.

Prior to the ninth century there was a widespread belief that evil witches existed, but by the 10th century the Catholic Church officially taught that witches didn't exist. In fact, it was heresy to say they were real. By about 975 there were some penalties for practicing witchcraft or using magic, but they were relatively mild. It appears that the church was building up to extreme punishments (torture and burning at the stake) when in the late thirteenth century Pope Innocent III approved a war of genocide against the Cathars (Gnostic Christians), whom he considered to be heretical. His successor, Pope Gregory IX, established the Inquisitional Courts to arrest, try, convict, and execute heretics. In 1326 the church began investigating witchcraft, and developed the theory of *demonology* as the origin of witchcraft that quickly expanded into the belief that witches swore allegiance to Satan. Trials and executions began to include those accused of such. From 1550 to 1650 trials and executions reached a peak. For anyone interested in even more details about this dark history, I recommend *The Witch Hunt in Early Modern Europe*, by Brian P. Levack, and *The Social and Cultural Context of European Witchcraft*, by Briggs and Robins.

In America, the Salem witchcraft trials in the late seventeenth century resulted in 19 executions and 150 accusations of witchcraft. There were a few other trials and executions in other parts of New England around the same time. Eventually, the voice of reason won out in the world, and in 1792 Poland executed the last person in Europe convicted of being a witch.

Astonishingly, there are still people who believe in witchcraft. In the mid 1990s, several hundred people, generally elderly women, accused of witchcraft in the northern province of South Africa, were lynched by frightened mobs. According to the website religioustolerance.org, in 1999 an American conservative Christian pastor called for a renewal of the burning times, to exterminate Wiccans and other Neopagans.

No wonder there's an underlying fear within our collective unconscious of being persecuted or even killed for believing in or practicing something different from what the powerful ones espouse. No rational person can say it will *never* happen again because it still does. I can't promise 100 percent safety when I'm trying to help a client release fear. But, I can say to my clients and readers with conviction that it is highly unlikely that in your lifetime, given where you live and who you are, that there will be anything but appreciation for you if you share your healing gifts. We need our healers. Every one of you.

It is often enough just to realize where it all began. Once you see how the limiting belief was created, your adult-evolved-self can replace that belief with a self-affirming and life-affirming new one.

Chapter 14

Spirit Attachments and Spirit Babies: Somebody Else's Fear

As for theories [regarding spirit attachments], I've come through the stages of cautious doubt, incredulity, and then amazement, to a casual, almost a shoulder-shrugging acceptance of those entities as being just what they say they are. Another indication is the astonishment of the clients: "Where did all that come from? Why did I say that name? I don't know anyone by that name! Did I make all that up?" The efforts of psychology and psychiatry to explain the experiences in other ways seem far more complicated and tortuous than simply accepting what the entities themselves say they are—not multiple personalities but obsessing [or possessing] minds or souls.

Louise Ireland-Frey, MD
quoted in *Regression Therapy, by Winafred Blake Lucas*

"I hear voices. I don't mean like I'm psychotic or anything, it seems like my own thoughts but it doesn't seem like me. It's kind of freaking me out." A new client, Alan, sober for three months, wanted help dealing with all the feelings that were coming up, perhaps because he could no longer numb them with gin.

"Maybe it's just that I'm still craving alcohol, but it's weird. I feel like there's someone else living inside my head with me."

He was not psychotic, not in withdrawal, and on no medication. His relationship was strong, he had a good job, and was well respected in the community. A normal guy. I decided to apply Occam's Razor: The notion that the simplest explanation of a problem is the preferred explanation, unless it is known to be wrong, and because like Dr. Ireland-Frey, quoted above, I'd dealt with this issue many times before meeting Alan. The simplest explanation was that there probably *was* someone else's voice inside his head. I didn't tell him anything about spirit attachments, but rather led him into a light trance and asked him if he could make contact with that voice.

He was quiet for a couple of minutes and then said, "I'm not sure I hear the voice, but I think I'm seeing something. A guy."

"Describe him," I said.

"Scruffy looking. You know, old clothes with patches, a three-day beard. I feel like if he was sitting here, he'd smell bad."

"Ask him his name."

"Really? This seems weird. Okay, I asked him. He says his name is Gilbert."

"Gilbert," I said, "how old are you?"

"He says, 'old enough to know better, sister.'"

I laughed. I was pretty sure I knew what was going on. I asked how long he'd been attached to Alan and, speaking through Alan, he said he thought about a dozen years. I asked him where he'd found Alan, and he said, "the boy's favorite bar, the one he'd walk to after work."

"What happened to you? What happened to your own body?" I asked. He wasn't sure. He knew Alan's body wasn't his, and that he must have died but he wasn't sure how. He said he'd been homeless since World War II and the last thing he remembered was lying down in a shop doorway in Portland's Old Town (where the homeless still congregate) on a very cold night in January. Alan wasn't the first live person he'd attached himself to. He hung around the bars and attached onto friendly drunk guys, but he'd stuck with Alan for a long time because his life was interesting.

Alan said, "He's upset that I've stopped drinking and he's been trying to talk me into going back to the bar. That's the voice I've been hearing. *I need a drink,*' he keeps saying."

I explained to Alan about spirit attachments (also called *entities* and sometimes *ghosts*). There are certain people who after death fail to make their transition into the afterlife. There are three reasons for this:

1. They are asleep or unconscious at the time of death and once they are out of their body they don't realize they are dead, like Gilbert. Unable to find his living body to return to, Gilbert was frightened and confused and quickly attached his energetic body, mind, or spirit to a compatible energy, in his case another alcoholic.

2. Sometimes the cause of death is violent and the victim has already left their body (dissociated) prior to death, like what I described happened to Nonie in chapter nine. She was captured by enemy soldiers, brutally raped, and her body hacked to pieces. Being out of her body at the time of death created confusion. Instead of attaching to another

body, Nonie's spirit remained in a familiar place although still lost and confused.

3. Sudden death, like in an explosion, war, or to a fetus or infant, will also create confusion and problems with transition.

Alan said it made sense, given what had just happened to him. Then he asked, "What next?"

"Now Gilbert gets some therapy," I said. I asked if he'd heard what I told Alan, and Alan replied, "He says he gets it." We explained to Gilbert that by clinging to his old ways and onto Alan he was wasting an opportunity to start over with a new life. I also made it clear that Alan did not want him around any longer. Gilbert was a little hurt, but after asking a few more questions about the process of crossing over, agreed to go. I asked for a Being to come and help him, and Alan said he watched him move into a bright light.

Spirit attachments, if they are present, will almost always show up right at the beginning of one's first regression session. It's like they are saying, "I'm the second strongest energy in the body, and you can't get by me without noticing my presence."

It makes sense that when one decides to go inside to look around, they would encounter what *isn't* themselves. You'd think entities would hide rather than reveal their presence, but fortunately for everyone's sake, they are easily discovered. It usually happens as clients are deepening their trance state by moving down inner stairs, escalators, or elevators, or just as they are stepping into the past. What's a little perverse about it is that most of the people I work with have no prior experience with hypnosis or regression and are somewhat anxious about what to expect. To be met by what might logically be called a ghost can be quite unnerving!

Mai came to see me about her generalized anxiety and a fear of being left. Like most new clients, she had little idea of what to expect. I explained there is a learning curve to having a good regression. At first she tried to control the situation by *trying* to see certain things. Eventually, with lots of encouragement, she got to a place where she saw a light ahead. Finally through the tunnel, she reported hearing crying. Then she began to weep. When I asked, "Who is crying?" Mai said, "She's little, maybe five."

"What do you hear when I ask *what's your name?*" I said.

"Becky?" Mai answered tentatively.

"Becky, hello, you're five years old, is that right? Will you tell us why you are sad?"

Mai whispered, "She's sad because she died." I asked Mai if she knew any-one named Becky who died at age five and she said *no*. I then asked her to use her intuition to determine if Becky was a past life of hers or the spirit of a little girl who has been following her around for a while, perhaps attached to her. She said it felt more like the latter.

I asked, "Becky, what happened to *your* body?" Suddenly Mai became very pale. I commented, "Oh my gosh, all the color drained from your face."

"She's telling me her mother got killed." We asked Becky if she died at the same time, and Mai thought not.

"Sweetheart, did you die alone?" I asked. Mai nodded yes. I asked how long she'd been attached to Mai and Becky said "a long time."

"What do you like about Mai?" I asked.

"She's nice."

I knew that Mai was a nurse, and wondered if Becky had died in the hos-pital and had attached there. After all, the hospital is an environment where there can be quite a few spirits walking up and down the halls.

"I don't feel that it was in a hospital. I think she was killed."

"Murdered."

"Yes."

"Sweetheart, do you know who killed you?" I could tell from looking at Mai that Becky did know. Weeping, Mai said it was Becky's father. He killed her mother first, then Becky.

Mai very tenderly whispered, "Becky thought she was a bad girl, and that's why daddy got so violent." Mai very quickly and with great compassion set the child straight. Once we had given Becky the attention and information she needed to understand she was innocent of any wrong doing, we asked her if she was ready to go to heaven (a concept most children understand best) and she said she wanted to be with her mom. We invited her mother to come and fetch her home. Mai wept, and said goodbye to Becky.

As we processed the experience later, she said she had mistaken Becky's anxiety and guilt as her own. After Becky's energy was cleansed from Mai's body, she said she felt lighter, relieved, and less anxious. There was more work to do around her fears of being left, but she was off to a very good start.

Are spirit attachments real?

Results from experiments are highly suggestive that consciousness lives on in some fashion after death, and individuals who have died and come back to life, usually after resuscitation, offer fascinating accounts, such as neurosurgeon, Eben Alexander in his bestselling book *Proof of Heaven*. These reports have come to be called near-death experiences or NDEs. These individuals say that what happened to them convinced them that consciousness exists after death.

There have been innumerable reports of patients fully anesthetized during surgery, who later gave specific details of what happened while they were unconscious. They often reported floating above their bodies. The details they provided were confirmed by those present. Many perfectly sane individuals report visits from recently departed friends and relatives.

After much investigation, neuroscientist Mario Beauregard concluded, "NDE studies also suggest that after physical death, mind, and consciousness may continue in a transcendent level of reality that is normally not accessible to our senses and awareness. This view is utterly incompatible with the belief of many materialists that the material world is the only reality."

Of course, if one believes in reincarnation, it goes without saying that one believes consciousness does not die when the body does. So when I encounter disembodied spirits in sessions, I'm quite prepared to work with that form of consciousness.

Who is vulnerable to attachments?

Alan had the unfortunate experience of having a spirit attach to his energy field, much like a parasite. Gilbert used some of Alan's energy, and urged him to keep drinking because that's what Gilbert craved. People who hang out in bars or drink to excess are vulnerable to attachment. It seems that one's energy field is weakened by drugs and alcohol, and the spirits of dead alcoholics, if they don't make the transition, tend to hang out at their favorite places.

Hospitals, nursing homes, and hospices predictably tend to have confused spirits present, and those who live, visit, or work there are vulnerable to attachments. It's a good idea to check your energy field from time to time to be sure you are the only spirit in your body.

If you think you have an attachment, consider seeking help from someone who does energy work, shamanic healing, or an experienced hypnotherapist.

Born with attachments

So what has this topic to do with being born scared? It's bad enough to pick up an attachment or two or more as an adult. But what happens if you are born with an attachment? After I presented the module on working with attachments during an intermediate course for past-life regression facilitators, I asked for a volunteer to help me demonstrate the process of identifying and working with them. This student threw her hand in the air and said, "As you were talking about this I started to feel very agitated. I'm pretty sure I've got one."

Mary was right. As she visualized going down stairs she reported someone was walking beside her.

"He was with me in our mother's womb, but he didn't survive. He's been with me ever since. Oh my god! He's the one who pushed me into the motor. He's responsible for other accidents and attacks on my health. He's angry that I survived and he didn't. He's the one who makes me feel like I don't deserve to feel joy. He makes me feel selfish, and he has caused me to sabotage my own success. Wow, he's the voice that says eat more and more."

It would be easy to think Mary was looking for an excuse for being accident prone, for having low self-esteem, depression, and a compulsion to overeat. But if this spirit was real and as powerful as she described, getting free of him would result in a quick turnaround of those problems.

We worked with Roger, expressing sympathy that he didn't survive to be her twin brother. His underlying fear of *not existing* had turned into anger he took out on his sister. When he finally felt heard and understood, he apologized to Mary. He did not want to proceed into the light, as we've come to think of it. Instead, Mary said, "He reluctantly departed toward a place he could be free, feel the wind on him, a grassy plain where he could run and be joyful."

Baby attachments: the scared unborn

I'm occasionally asked my position on abortion. Let me show you how I came to believe what I do.

This woman's parents were self-proclaimed hippies and raised her to be a free spirit and a feminist. She was sexually adventurous and pro-choice in her politics. She was against birth control pills because of the health risks, and therefore she found herself pregnant—often. Not wanting to be a mother, with each pregnancy Darlene had an abortion.

She sought my help because of anxiety. She'd had a couple of mild panic attacks and her boyfriend was worried about her sleepless nights and occasional sleepwalking episodes. I knew nothing about her sexual history this first session.

As she started to relax and go into a trance state, she said she felt as if she was spinning. It was unpleasant. She thought she might throw up. I tried something that often works; I asked, "Who is worried?" She took a deep breath and said something was changing. "I feel like there's a voice inside that wants to answer that."

"Good. Let's create a safe place for us to have a conversation." I encouraged her to relax deeper, and then when she was ready, to walk into the safe place.

"I'm trying to get in the door, but there are all these hands grabbing at me. I don't like this."

"This could be important, will you stay with me? Look at the hands that are grabbing you. Ask what they want."

"They want me. There are all these babies. Some are crying. What does this mean?" It could have been imagery of inner children, parts of herself wanting attention, but my intuition led me to ask:

"Darlene, have you ever been pregnant?"

"Yes, several times."

"Do you have kids?"

"No, I had abortions."

"How many babies are in this room?

"Seven." She turned pale and put both hands over her mouth. She whispered, "I've had seven abortions."

I told Darlene what I'd learned years ago from one of the founders of the Association for Past-Life Research and Therapies, the late Dr. Winafred Blake Lucas. I took a seminar from her called, "Conversations with the Unborn." She often quoted Dr. Gladys McGarey, internationally recognized as the Mother of holistic medicine. "If we look at life as a continuum, which the concept of reincarnation enables us to do, then a soul is not destroyed when an abortion is performed. A soul, entering into the earth plane at this time, is a being that has had prior existence and will have existence after this. This is not the only life, and if an abortion is performed, this is not the end for an entity, and it will not result in its losing a chance to express itself."

In that context, Dr. Lucas taught us to have a conversation with the soul of the infant. That conversation could take place prior to conception, during pregnancy, if an abortion is contemplated or decided upon; after a miscarriage or fetal death; or in Darlene's case, after an abortion, if the spirit has remained attached to the mother.

Darlene could not deny her own inner experience. All seven souls of those she had aborted had remained. Some were angry; most were confused and scared. Perhaps it was their feelings she was experiencing.

"What can I do?" she asked.

"We'll have a conversation with each one. You explain why you made the decision you did, tell each one, if it is true, that you didn't realize a soul existed with the pregnancy, and anything else that comes to you. Speak through your heart. See if they have any questions, too."

It was a very emotional conversation. Internally, Darlene asked them to sit in a circle, and she spoke to each in turn. Many did have questions and she answered them. She wept as she apologized for her carelessness, and for their fear and pain. When they were finished, we told them they could go now, returning to source, where they would be helped to choose a new mother and continue their journey. One little boy said he still wanted Darlene for a mother, if she would have him. She said yes to him. They all left, but the boy said he would see her soon.

What remained was for Darlene to forgive herself. "I will. Soon, but not today. I need to sit with this for now."

At her next session she reported feeling great, sleeping well, anxiety free, but changed forever. "I'm much more mindful about everything. I found myself looking at babies, and I realized there is a lot of consciousness even in a newborn. I've got a lot of growing up to do, but my boyfriend and I are seriously talking about marriage and raising that little boy together."

Pro-Life and Pro-Choice

As one who believes our consciousness endures and that we do reincarnate, I find myself both pro-life and pro-choice. My experience with pre-birth memories informs me that the soul is present, possibly even before, or right at conception, and that soul deserves love and respect. But, as Drs. McGarey and Lucas taught with great compassion, an abortion can be the best choice for both mother and child. In earlier chapters, I've explained how an unwanted baby knows it is unwanted, even prior to birth. That knowledge results in future mental and emotional problems, higher instances of crib death, anti-social behavior, and suicide. There are many reasons a woman may make the difficult choice of abortion, and it is her right. However, that choice should never be made lightly, and never without having a conversation with the soul of the fetus who also has rights.

I heard a story from the Japanese tradition about how an indigenous tribe would prepare to cut down a tree. The day before, they would talk to the tree and explain what they were about to do. They would give thanks to the tree, and then make a small cut in the bark, thereby giving the spirit of the tree an opportunity to leave and be spared the pain of its destruction. That same respect should be given to any living thing, especially one with the sentience of a spirit baby.

When I work with a woman who has made the decision to terminate a pregnancy, I lead her into a light trance state, and then invite the spirit of the child to join us. Some women simply imagine this conversation, but most of those I've worked with feel the presence, and sometimes see the child in their mind's eye. The woman explains her decision, and then asks the spirit to comment.

There's no *one way* this goes. Sometimes the spirit is upset and angry, but more often than not, it understands and will go willingly. Sometimes they make an agreement to try again at some future time; sometimes the spirit decides it will choose another mother or set of parents. We never end the conversation until there is peace between the two. I've gotten calls after this process telling me that before my client could have the abortion, the baby left on its own—a miscarriage occurred. The best possible outcome of a very difficult situation, in my opinion.

Chapter 15

Change Your Beliefs and Change Your Life

You made it through the book. I imagine for some of you it was a bit of a roller coaster, because you likely identified with at least one and probably many of the causes of anxiety and fears within yourself or a loved one. If you have been triggered, you have both my sympathy and congratulations because that means you have unburied something you have repressed, and you are on your way to discovering the root cause of anxiety or a fear. If your anxiety has greatly increased, make notes of the topics and issues that stimulated those increased feelings and take them to your next therapy session. If you don't have a therapist, I urge to you consider looking for one who is open to a holistic (non-pharmaceutical) approach. If your anxiety and fears are mild, what follows is the three-step approach I use in my office that might help you to help yourself.

Step One: Find the Cause.

Anxiety and fears have their roots in past trauma, with these exceptions: anxiety caused by medical reasons such as neurological illnesses; cardiopulmonary, degenerative and endocrine disorders; or toxins and drugs (prescription, over-the-counter, stimulants). Whether physical, emotional, or mental in origin, the roots of anxiety can be discovered. With that discovery you can begin to heal. This is not to say that you begin with awareness of trauma. You might, but usually that awareness is so deeply buried or hidden from you that all you know at first are your symptoms. That's why hypnosis is my preferred method of conscious investigation. Sometimes the past reveals itself in a flashback or a vivid dream, but usually it takes the safety of a professional's office for someone to be able to relax, turn down the left-brain chatter, and focus all his or her attention inward. However, some people are able to use self-hypnosis to help themselves. There are recordings to help with this process including my own, which is listed in the appendix.

You can also assume that in your identification with others who have similar symptoms to your own, that the cause is likely similar to theirs. In that way you can use that as a springboard to step 2. For instance, if you were strongly affected by the chapter on womb twin survivors, and even if you don't have confirmation of that from your mother, your identification with survivors means you could heal those same symptoms the way they did.

For an excellent list of the medical reasons for anxiety and alternatives to prescription drugs, I recommend *Complementary and Alternative Treatments in Psychiatry 2012,* by Stradford, Vickar, Berger, Cass, available as a free e-book at www.flyingpublisher.com or as a print copy at Amazon.

Step Two: Evaluate Your Beliefs.

After the cause is discovered (or presumed), the next step is the realization of what beliefs came from the primary cause. The *beliefs that developed as a result of the trauma* cause the most trouble. In chapter one, when the pre-born girl heard the sounds, including her mother's screams when her father was attacked, several negative beliefs were formed: *The world is a dangerous place, it is my job to not add to my father's pain or my mother's burden, but rather to make them feel better.* As a result she was in constant fear of attack, and put the well being of even strangers before her own. Her healing took place as she recognized those beliefs were not true, and replaced them with what was true.

In chapter two, because of his conception by rape, the pre-born boy believed he was the source of his mother's pain and his own rejection, and decided he should never have been born.

Chapter three has a version of that same theme, but with a twist. This infant was stuck in the womb, and then experienced panic when things got critical, and then felt relief when delivered by C-section. This cycle created a belief in the form of what we call repetition compulsion: *This is the way my world works: you get stuck and then you get rescued.*

In chapter nine, you read of a woman who as a teen had an out-of-body experience while taking LSD. The terror of feeling like she was going to be lost in space and never return to her body threw open the past-life memory of that very thing happening. The initial experience of being lost in time and space created a belief in her current life: *I could get so far from home I'd never get back.* The panic attacks she experienced after the drug experience were triggered by imperceptible reminders of the initial trauma, and then came the final belief, which led to agoraphobia, *I'm only truly safe at home.*

As Bruce Lipton so aptly put it, "The subconscious memory system is very partial to rapidly downloading and emphasizing perceptions regarding things in your environment that are threatening to life and limb." He reminds us that the gigantic repository of beliefs we call the subconscious has no system that separates fact from fiction. And we make most decisions based upon beliefs.

Once you have discovered the initial trauma, and then determined the beliefs you reached about the initial trauma—including the reactions of yourself and others—then you can examine those beliefs under the watchful eye of your adult, rational, and I hope *patient* and *compassionate* self. Some of the beliefs we looked at in this book were dispelled in this way.

Is the world a dangerous place? If that is your belief, consider this: Right here and now as you read these words, are you in danger? The fact is we are safer now than ever in history, although if you watch cable "news" programs you may be convinced otherwise. If you want a counter argument to mainstream media, I recommend reading Daniel Gardner's book, *The Science of Fear: How the Culture of Fear Manipulates Your Brain*, or Gregg Easterbrook's book, *The Progress Paradox: How Life Gets Better While People Feel Worse.* Easterbrook reminds us that we are better off than kings and queens of bygone days, with our indoor plumbing, safe drinking water, and penicillin. Sadly, the greatest danger to some people is their own beliefs. For instance, the greatest number of gun deaths is by suicide.

Other beliefs *dispelled* by my client's adult selves:

- A preborn infant is responsible for his or her mother's feelings—positive and negative.
- A child conceived by rape should feel shame.
- An unplanned, unwanted baby will never be wanted or loved by anyone.
- Bad luck (failure, disappointment, etc.) is the story of my life.

Step Three: Replace Old Beliefs.

Each limiting or untrue belief is replaced with a new truth:

- I'm responsible for my own wellbeing.
- I love and esteem myself.

- I am loved and lovable.
- I'm entitled to live a rich and full life—I'm in charge of my own story.

These are not just affirmations, although they may feel like that in the beginning. Changing old beliefs takes effort—repetition, and good old "fake it 'till you make it." As positive thoughts accumulate in the subconscious, they will crowd out the negative. As I tell my clients, *beliefs in the form of memories are created by* repetition *or by intensity. Either way, they are deeply imbedded and most are resistant to change. It is the repetition of replacement beliefs that results in change. Sometimes it happens in an instant, but often the ruts are too deep. Think of your subconscious negative beliefs as an enormous steamship on the ocean. You need to turn that ship around. It won't turn quickly because of its size, but persistence will pay off, and soon you'll realize you are moving in a new direction.*

In the appendix you'll find descriptions of some of the therapies I and other holistic therapists use. Some of them lend themselves to self-help and healing.

As Fred Alan Wolf, the quantum physicist in the movie *What the Bleep Do We Know*, has often said, imagination supplies the building blocks of reality —our universal reality and our personal reality.

Use the power of your own imagination and you truly can re-create your own reality—body, mind, and spirit. And remember, the subconscious does not easily discern the difference between imagination and outer reality. That's how much power you have to scare yourself sick or to heal from anxiety and fear.

Acknowledgments

I've had a blessed life, and a much more interesting one that I would have designed on my own, especially for having been born and raised in a small conservative town in Idaho. There I colored inside the lines and was taught not to question authority. The experience that helped me break free of rigid thinking was graduate school. How I got selected to participate in that experimental and highly funded program to train therapists at Arizona State University, I'll never know. We were thirty-three people selected from all over the country, and we were taught by some of the best and brightest of those breaking away from tradition. We were immersed in a variety of emerging ideas, and made to carefully examine ourselves through group therapy and encounter groups. Coloring outside the lines was exhilarating. My first thank you is to Professor McGreevy, and the faculty of the Counseling Institute, class of 1968.

A good education is a great foundation, but next comes experience. For that, I express gratitude to the directors and staff at the High Plains Community Mental Health Center, Hays, Kansas, where for three years I worked on the inpatient psychiatric unit. This center was founded and directed by group of people who were visionaries, and we therapists enjoyed extraordinary in-house training, including psychodrama, testing, and hypnosis.

But the people who have shaped my career and taught me the most are my clients—the ones who stuck with me as I was learning my craft, especially, but to all of them, for their courage to face their problems, their tenacity to keep working when it was painful, and who let me walk with them to the other side, beyond survival and into wholeness.

As for **Born Scared**, being the author of two spiritual books (then called New Age) I worried that I would not be able to cross over into psychology and be taken seriously. It took the encouragement and support of several friends and fellow writers to decide to make the effort. So thanks to Kate Holder, from my Tucson writer's group, a professional writer and political analyst with a great head on her shoulders, who read my outline and a few early chapters. She gave me both suggestions and encouragement. Thanks to Gordon Simmons, longtime friend and practical visionary, who did the same. Thanks also to my short-lived writer's group in Portland for their thoughtful critiques, especially those who found the concepts within the book challenging (that was very helpful): Brenda Stevens, Sue Ceswick, Nancy Olson-Chatalas, and Kayle Sandberg-Lewis. I'm especially grateful to Kayle, who read most of the book with the red pencil of a good editor and the knowledge of a brain specialist (she teaches neurofeedback techniques at National College of Natural Medicine, in Portland, OR).

Finally, thanks to Elizabeth Lyon, author and editor. I had used Elizabeth's popular *Nonfiction Book Proposals Anybody Can Write* as a template for my proposal for *The Lost Sisterhood* in 2000, and when it was time to pitch *Born Scared*, I decided to call on the best for help. To my delight, she agreed to take me on, and it has been her steadfast belief in the book and her generous friendship that has brought me to the finish line. As she wrote in her own acknowledgments: "Every writer needs a good editor." How true.

Appendix

Healing techniques and practices mentioned in *Born Scared*:

Amino acid therapy

Amino acids play central roles as building blocks of proteins and in regulating metabolism. When it comes to moods, we focus on the acids that make neurotransmitters. I call it how the body talks to the mind, and vice versa. Of the twenty amino acids required by humans, we manufacture ten of them, and must get the other ten (which are called the essential amino acids) from food or supplements. The body doesn't store them, so we need a daily intake. A deficiency can result in anxiety, depression, loss of mental focus, sleep disturbance, muscle tension, and a lack of joy. There are no side effects from taking the supplements (although rarely someone will not tolerate one), and many of these work as well or better than prescription anti-depressants and tranquilizers. Holistic MDs and naturopaths can determine which amino acids are deficient, and make recommendations, or you can often figure it yourself by using the information in Julia Ross's books, *The Diet Cure* and *The Mood Cure*, and Dr. Daniel Amen's, *Change Your Brain, Change Your Life.*

Brain Gym

A non-profit educational corporation, the program uses intentional movement to optimize learning. The core movements and activities according to their website: " … recall the movements naturally done during the first years of life when learning to coordinate the eyes, ears, hands, and whole body … and that the interdependence of movement, cognition, and applied learning is the basis of their work. Clients, teachers, and students have been reporting for over twenty years on the effectiveness of these simple activities on concentration, focus, memory, academics, physical coordination, relationships, self-responsibility, organization skills, and attitude."

Cognitive Behavioral Therapy (CBT), Dialectical Behavioral Therapy (DBT)

CBT is what it sounds like, a process designed to help clients examine their thinking—to see how it contributes to their suffering, and to their actions and reactions (behavior). Clients are given tools to help them change their thinking and to regulate their reactions to people and events. Almost all therapists will use this process during the course of working with a client.

DBT is a form of cognitive therapy, but with a great deal of structure. It was initially developed to help those diagnosed with Borderline Personality Disorder, now used with anyone who reacts with great intensity, often extreme, within interpersonal relationships and who take longer than normal to return to a baseline feeling. Dialectic is by definition about using reason to arrive at a conclusion. In psychology it is more about looking at the ways in which there is tension between opposites like love and hate, right and wrong, with me or against me, and the trouble people get into with black and white thinking. DBT takes work and is best done in a hospital or clinic setting where there is a combination of education, therapy, practicing new ways of thinking and reacting, and a very well-trained staff.

Creative visualization

From the bestseller of the same name, by Shakti Gawain, published in 1997, *Creative Visualization* is a combination of meditation practice, affirmations, and spiritual guidance, such as how to connect with guides, your higher self, etc. I've used one of her brief affirmations over and over with my clients " … this, or something better." Shaki said people ask for too little and think too small about their own potential.

Dialogue

A process in which a therapist facilitates a conversation between the client and others. Sometimes it is called *"parts work,"* and consists of having an inner conversation between your adult and child selves; you with another person (dead or alive), or with your array of roles—father, brother, boss, neighbor, musician. Sometimes it is called *"the empty chair"*; in this case you imagine the *other* sitting in a chair opposite you. It is useful to switch places during the conversation, to gain insight into another's point of view.

Eye Movement Desensitization and Reprocessing (EMDR) aka Rapid Eye Therapy

First developed in 1987 by Francine Shapiro, a clinical psychologist, when she noticed that moving her eyes rapidly from side to side reduced the intensity of a disturbing thought or memory. Over the years she developed a process for helping others, and has since then trained numerous therapists in its use. While some critics claim it is really a form of exposure and desensitization therapy and the eye movements are irrelevant, results speak for themselves. This therapy is now widely used in the treatment of post-traumatic stress disorder with veterans, rape victims, and other traumatized individuals, including children. This is the best choice when you know where your trauma came from and you want to be free of the emotional impact.

Guided imagery

Sometimes called Interactive Guided Imagery, it is a powerful therapeutic process that affects a client's mental images. I learned the basics of this process in a workshop with David Bresler and Martin Rossman, founders of The Academy for Guided Imagery. This definition is from their website: "*The term 'guided imagery' refers to a wide variety of techniques, including simple visualization and direct suggestion using imagery, metaphor and story-telling, fantasy exploration and game playing, dream interpretation, drawing, and active imagination where elements of the unconscious are invited to appear as images that can communicate with the conscious mind.*" www.academyforguidedimagery.com

Hypnotherapy

I like the description from Wikipedia: "A form of psychotherapy utilized to create unconscious change in the patient in the form of new responses, thoughts, attitudes, behaviors and/or feelings. It is undertaken with a subject in hypnosis. A person who is hypnotized displays certain unusual characteristics and propensities, compared with a non-hypnotized subject, most notably heightened suggestibility and responsiveness."

Hypnosis is my most valuable tool. The process quiets the mind, shuts off the inner critic, and allows the client to access inner material, hidden memories, negative beliefs, and also their own inner courage, strength, and wisdom. Being suggestible is useful. Taking in positive suggestions is often life changing for people. It is safe in the hands of a trained professional, and even with a poorly trained one, clients will never accept a suggestion to do something that is against their own principles.

The practice of hypnotherapy took a huge hit in the 1990s over the issue of false memories, and some reactionaries demonized the entire profession. Many organizations reacted by shutting down hypnotherapy. It is true that in a highly suggestible state, a careless or manipulative hypnotist could plant a picture that becomes integrated into the subconscious as real. (I prefer the term subconscious to unconscious. The terms are used interchangeably, but unconscious suggests there is no access to the memory.) A well-trained hypnotherapist avoids this problem by not ask leading questions. An example of a leading question and how false memories are created is, "Was it your teacher? Did she have you ... (fill in the blank)? Were there pictures of ...? When we hear something, our mind responds by picturing it. If an authority figure asks, *was it your teacher?* you will automatically picture your teacher. If you are asked, *were there pictures of such and such,* you will picture such and such.

Unfortunately, many threw the baby out with the bath and this powerful and valuable tool is still met with suspicion by some. However, we are making a comeback as more people discover the benefits. What I've heard from clients who've had years of talk therapy, or tried numerous drugs without much benefit, is that hypnotherapy took them deeper into themselves than they could have imagined possible, and that as a result of the process they were finally healed.

Inner child therapy

A process of assisting the client to connect with his or her most vulnerable parts of the self. Two therapists who brought the concept into popularity are Charles Whitfield and John Bradshaw. Bradshaw was greatly inspired by the works of Alice Miller, who wrote *The Drama of the Gifted Child* and *For Your Own Good: Hidden Cruelty in Child-Rearing and the Roots of Violence.*

If clients react to their own inner kids with loving kindness, I know their prognosis for healing is good. Women tend to have an easier time communicating with their vulnerable inner "parts," but most of the men I work with respond quite positively as well. Severely abused adults will often feel estranged from their little selves, and even reject them in the beginning, using the same words they heard—*he or she is stupid, weak, dirty, no good.*

Past-life regression

A process in which a therapist or facilitator assists a person, generally via hypnosis, to access the part of their mind which can remember prior lifetimes. While tapping into past lives will sometimes happen spontaneously—there are incidences of people reporting memories of past lives throughout history—the process became more formalized when in the late 1950s, therapists began to recognize the healing effects of simply finding the origin—in their client's past—of a present-day problem.

With better training in hypnosis, and the common practice of regressing patients/clients back to early childhood experiences, an increasing number of therapists were finding past lives being reported. Dr. Ronald Jue and a distinguished group of psychiatrists, psychologists, and social workers founded the Association for Past-Life Research and Therapies in California in 1980. They held conferences, workshops, and offered training in the process. I joined that association in the late 1980s and benefited greatly, not just from what I learned, but also from the relationships that developed. That association is now called the International Association for Past-Life Research and Therapies (IARRT). www.iarrt.org/

Many people were introduced to the process with the publication of psychiatrist Brian Weiss' bestselling book, *Many Lives, Many Masters*. Dr. Weiss helped to "normalize" regression as a valid therapeutic tool.

Post-hypnotic suggestion

Instructing the client's conscious and subconscious mind to think in more positive ways, and to increase their will power, courage, and determination after they leave the therapy session.

Present-time reality

A process in which the client is assisted to update his or her information about their world. Most, if not all, trauma that is affecting them in the present happened in the past yet there are parts of themselves still trapped in the past. Instead of reliving past trauma, the client envisions bringing the traumatized self into the present where they are adults (or *bigger* kids) with power, options, and the ability to ask for and receive help. People who regress deeply into a child state often need to be reminded what year it is and where they are.

Progression therapy

A hypnotherapy/guided visualization technique for helping a client access an image or story of a potential future. First described by past-life regression pioneer, Helen Wambach, PhD, and featured in a book by Chet B. Snow, PhD, entitled *Mass Dreams of the Future* (1989), they used the same process as we use in taking people back in time, but instead they moved people forward in time. A fun project, they collected data from 2,500 volunteers progressed in groups by a number of therapists throughout the country. While the data was interesting, the whole concept of being able to predict the future is brought into serious question, because some of the dates of events "seen" have come and gone and those things reported were not even close to reality. With all due respect to Drs. Snow and Wambach for their contributions to past-life regression therapy, their primary message about the future is beneficial: it could get worse or it could get better and it is up to us to determine which.

I simply say to clients in progressions, you can access a potential future, but don't expect to reliably predict the future. Also, the material that shows up may be a symbolic story requiring interpretation, just as we interpret dreams.

Progressions can be used in a very positive way, especially when working with addicts who *cannot imagine* life without their drugs of choice, or heart-broken clients who *can't imagine* a life without someone they have lost, or those who feel powerless and *can't imagine* ever feeling powerful. As with most of the therapies described in this appendix, which attest to the power of imagery, taking charge of your imagery—changing it by seeing how you want your life to be—changes your brain, your beliefs, and actions and reactions. The addict can see a future of sobriety, the heart-broken one can imagine a future of acceptance and moving on, the powerless one can picture doing things with effectiveness. Believing is seeing; seeing is believing.

Rebirthing

There is one form of rebirthing which utilizes a rapid breathing technique to push memories and emotions to the surface. In the hands of a trained rebirther, this can be a very powerful experience. While it may have begun as a way to help release the trauma of a difficult birth, it is now useful for all types of emotional issues.

Shamans may use a process called soul retrieval that involves variations on the theme of rebirthing. The process varies among the many traditions, but in simple terms the idea is the healer assists the client by removing energies that do not belong in the body, and bringing back into the body any parts of the self that were split off due to illness, trauma, or outside interference.

In my practice I assist a client who had a traumatic birth or an abusive childhood to imagine a positive new birth. Under hypnosis, clients picture a calm and peaceful environment and invite into the birthing space only those who love them and are glad they were born. There's no formula for how this works, as it is a co-created experience, but the idea is that by the end of the process, clients embrace their infant-self and promise to take care of him or her with loving kindness. Self-love, which includes self-care and self-nurturing, is easier when you think of it as taking care of the precious child within yourself.

Reframing

This technique may have originated with the brilliant hypnotherapist Milton H. Erickson; at least that's where I first heard the term. The concept became more formalized via a therapy known as Neuro Linguistic Programming (NLP). The idea behind it is that much anxiety and suffering comes not so much from events as the *context and meaning* one gives the event. Reframing is about looking at the meaning and mentally changing either the context or the meaning, or both, so that the client feels empowered and positive. A classic book on the topic is *Reframing: Neuro-Linguistic Programming and the Transformation of Meaning,* by Richard Bandler and John Grinder.

Tapping

One of the techniques in the growing field of energy psychology, the proper name of this process is Thought Field Therapy (TFT). It is a sequential tapping procedure developed by Dr. Roger Callahan, who says it balances the body's energy system to eliminate negative emotions and fears. When I first saw this demonstrated, I found it hard to believe such a simple process—using your fingers to tap on different parts of your face (some also include other parts of the body)—would do much, but I've found it to be very useful. It is one thing to think about self-forgiveness, and quite another to shift the energy of guilt and shame stored in the body. One well-known teacher of an outgrowth of Callahan's work is Gary Craig. At his website you'll find illustrations and scripts for his process, called The Emotional Freedom Technique (EFT), downloadable for free. www.emofree.com

Associations mentioned in *Born Scared*

Birth Psychology: The Association for Prenatal and Perinatal Psychology and Health (APPPAH), www.birthpsychology.com/

Founded by 1983 by Thomas Verny, MD, APPPAH is a public-benefit educational and scientific organization offering information, inspiration, and support to medical professionals, expecting parents, and all persons interested in expanding horizons of birth psychology. Membership has several levels, including those with a lay interest in the topic. Members receive a newsletter and enjoy an annual conference featuring leaders in the field.

IARRT-The International Association for Past-Life Research and Therapies, www.iarrt.org/

You'll find information on conferences for professionals, but normally open to the public, training programs leading to certification as a past-life regression therapist, research and journal articles, and a directory of members, if you are looking for a PLR therapist in your area.

Treatment programs

There are many fine programs across the country. I'm only recommending those that I have personally found to be excellent.

Addictions. Twelve-Step programs are free, member led, and have a structure and process that has proven itself over generations. There's one near you. An alternative to the 12 Steps is Rational Recovery, a smaller organization, but also effective, also member led and free. For those who can't make it with group support, residential treatment should be considered, and more states are coming around to making treatment a mandatory feature of all health insurance plans, and free for the uninsured.

Eating Disorders. When outpatient support is not enough, especially for anorexia, and bulimia, I personally recommend Mirasol, a residential treatment center in Tucson that combines medical, psychological, and spiritual approaches to recovery, in a very beautiful setting. They have programs for adult women and teenage boys and girls. www.mirasol.net/ For teenage boys and adult males, Rosewood Ranch is recommended. www.rosewoodranch.com.

Codependency, trauma, and addictions. It is rare to have a single disorder. Because I have deep respect for the founders of The Meadows (Pia Mellody, *Facing Codependency* and John Bradshaw, *Healing the Shame That Binds Us*, and many other books, when I have a client who just can't manage his or her life enough to benefit from outpatient services, including my own, I refer them to The Meadows, also in Arizona. www.themeadows.com/

Birth Trauma

For adults dealing with birth trauma, especially adult attachment disorder, and for intensive personal growth retreats with professional staff in attendance 24 hours a day, check out The Star Foundation 10-day retreats. The founder and director of this program is Barbara Findeisen, who was one of the founders of The Association for Past-life Research and Therapies, and has for many years been a leader in the Birth Psychology Association. www.starfound.org/

Recommended reading: adoption

- *Twenty Things Adopted Kids Wish Their Adoptive Parents Knew,* by Sherrie Eldridge.
- *Trauma Through a Child's Eyes: Awakening the Ordinary Miracle of Healing,* by Peter A. Levine, PhD, and Maggie Kline.
- *The Primal Wound: Understanding the Adopted Child,* by Nancy Newton Verrier.
- *Journey of the Adopted Self: A Quest for Wholeness,* by Betty Jean Lifton. Also by Lifton: *Twice Born: Memoirs of an Adopted Daughter,* and, *Lost and Found: The Adoption Experience.* After her death the New York Times reported: "Her searing condemnations of the secrecy that traditionally shrouded adoption became touchstones for adoptees throughout the world."

Recommended reading: anxious children

- *What to Do When You Worry Too Much: A Kid's Guide to Overcoming Anxiety* (What to Do Guides for Kids) by Dawn Heubner and Bonnie Matthews.
- Also recommended is the MindUp program developed by actress Goldie Hawn with a team of educators and neuroscientists: www.thehawnfoundation.org/

Bibliography

Alexander, Eben. Proof of Heaven: A Neurosurgeon's Journey into the Afterlife. Simon & Schuster, 2012.

Beauregard, Mario. *Brain Wars: The Scientific Battle Over the Existence of the Mind and the Proof That Will Change the Way We Live Our Lives.* HarperOne, 2013 [2012].

Biggs, Robin. *Witches & Neighbors: The Social and Cultural Center of European Witchcraft.* Penguin Books, 1998 [1996].

Bowman, Carol. *Children's Past Lives: How Past Life Memories Affect Your Child.* Bantam Books, 2012 [1997].

Chopra, Deepak, and Simon, David. *Magical Beginnings, Enchanted Lives: A Holistic Guide to Pregnancy and Childbirth.* Three Rivers Press, 2005.

Easterbrook, Gregg. *The Progress Paradox: How Life Gets Better While People Feel Worse.* Random House, 2004 [2003].

Gardner, Daniel. *The Science of Fear: How the Culture of Fear Manipulates Your Brain.* Plume/Penguin Group, 2009 [2008].

Grof, Stanislav. *Beyond The Brain: Birth, Death and Transcendence in Psychotherapy.* State University (NY) Press, 1985.

Grof, Stanislav. *Healing Our Deepest Wounds: The Holotropic Paradigm Shift.* Stream of Experience Productions, 2012.

Hunt, Douglas. *What Your Doctor May Not Tell You About Anxiety, Phobias, & Panic Attacks: The All-Natural Program That Can Help You Conquer Your Fears. Warner Books, 2009* [2005].

Karr-Morse, Robin, Wiley, Meredith S. *Ghosts from the Nursery: Tracing the Roots of Violence.* Atlantic Monthly Press, 2007 [1998].

Karr-Morse, Robin. Meredith Wiley. *Scared Sick: The Role of Childhood Trauma in Adult Disease.* Basic Books, 2012.

Lawson, Christine. *Understanding the Borderline Mother: Helping Her Children Transcend the Intense, Unpredictable, and Volatile Relationship. Jason Aronson, Inc, 2010* [2000].

Lipton, Bruce H. *The Biology of Belief: Unleashing the Power of Consciousness, Matter & Miracles.* Hay House, 2013 [2008].

Leininger, Bruce, and Leininger, Andrea. *Soul Survivor: The Reincarnation of a World War II Pilot.* Grand Central Publishing, 2010 [2009].

Levack, Brian P. *The Witch-Hunt in Early Modern Europe.* Pearson Education Limited, 1987, 3d ed, Pearson, 2006 [1989].

Lucas, Winafred Blake. *Regression Therapy: A Handbook for Professionals, (two volume set). Includes Past Life Therapy and Special Instances of Altered State Work.* Transpersonal Publishing, 2007 [1993].

Monroe, Robert. *Journeys Out of the Body, updated ed.* Broadway Books, 1992 [1971].

Moody, Raymond. *Life After Life: The Investigation of a Phenomenon—Survival of Bodily Death,* 25th anniversary ed. HarperOne, 2001.

Paul, Annie Murphy. *Origins: How the Nine Months Before Birth Shape the Rest of Our Lives.* Free Press, NY, 2011 [2010].

Roberts, Jane. *The Oversoul Seven Trilogy. Amber-Allen Publishing, 2012.* Originally published as The Education of Oversoul 7 [1973].

Ross, Julia, *The Mood Cure: The 4—Step Program to Take Charge of Your Emotions—Today.* Viking, 2003 [2002].

Schwartz, Gary E. *The Afterlife Experiments; Breakthrough Scientific Evidence of Life After Death.* Atria Books, 2003 [2002].

Verny, Thomas R., Weintraub, Pamela. *Pre-Parenting: Nurturing Your Child from Conception.* Simon & Schuster, 2003 [2002].

Verny, Thomas R., Kelly, John. *The Secret Life of the Unborn Child: How You Can Prepare Your Unborn Baby for a Happy, Healthy Life.* Dell Trade Paperback, 1982 [1981].

Verrier, Nancy Newton. *The Primal Wound: Understanding the Adopted Child.* Gateway Press, Inc., 2007 [1993].

Weiss, Brian. *Through Time Into Healing: Discovering the Power of Regression Therapy to Erase Trauma and Transform Mind, Body, and Relationships.* Touchstone/Simon & Schuster, 2012 [1992].

Whitaker, Robert. *Anatomy of an Epidemic: Magic Bullets, Psychiatric Drugs, and the Astonishing Rise of Mental Illness in America.* Broadway Books, 2011 [2010]

BRN SARED 127

Articles/Booklets/Research Cited

"Complementary Alternative Treatments in Psychiatry, 2012," Stadford, Vickar, Berger & Cass. Free online at www.operationflyingpublisher.com/pdf/FPG _008_ComplementaryandAlternativeMedicineTreatmentsinPsychiatry_2012 .pdf

Consciousness: For articles and research. www.noetic.org/

Eating disorders, national statistics: www.nationaleatingdisorders.org/general -statistics/

Green, Richard J., PhD, "How Many Witches?" http://www.holocaust-history .org/~rjg/witches.shtml/

Hayton, Althea. www.altheahayton.com/wombtwin/

Ingram, Julia, MA. *"How Mainstream Psychology is Missing the Mark,"* Blog, *May 21, 2013*, www.juliaingram.com/child-anxiety/

Moody, Raymond, MD. www.lifeafterlife.com/

Vanishing Twin Syndrome: www.americanpregnancy.org/multiples/vanishing-twin.html

Julia Ingram, MA. CD: *Help Yourself Overcome Fear*

27895958R00084

Made in the USA
Charleston, SC
25 March 2014